THE YORKSHIRE DALES

A common sight in the Dales fifty years ago. Herbert Bentham and his family are turning hay at Dockle Sike Farm, near Dent. Once dry, it would be led into the barn on a sledge. (Geoffrey N Wright)

THE YORKSHIRE DALES

A 50TH ANNIVERSARY CELEBRATION OF THE NATIONAL PARK

DAVID JOY

GREAT NORTHERN

Great Northern Books
PO Box 213, Ilkley, LS29 9WS

in association with the
Yorkshire Dales National Park Authority

ISBN: 0 9544002 7 5

Supported by the

Printed by
The Amadeus Press, Cleckheaton.

British Cataloguing in Publication Data
A catalogue for this book is available at the British Library

Contents

Foreword 7

Introduction 9

Part 1 Fifty Years Ago **11**

The Quiet Dales 13

Portrait of the 1950s 16

Part 2 The Changing Dales **31**

Fifty Years of Change 33

At Home in Swaledale 46

The Farming Scene 50

Three Generations in Coverdale 66

Travelling around the Dales: Then and Now 72

Enjoying the Yorkshire Dales 87

No Wind Farms, Please! 98

Part 3 The Dales Today **101**

Through the Year 103

Looking Ahead 121

From Four to Eleven 124

Subscribers 141

The Yorkshire Dales
Painting by David Hockney

"Wensleydale Creature", oil on canvas
© David Hockney 1997

Foreword

by Brian Blessed

President, Council for National Parks

When I was a child in the 1950s, I had a racing bike and used to cycle for a couple of days round the Dales. I still visit the area every three months and am astonished at the new spirit and speed of recovery following the Foot and Mouth outbreak. I intend to pour my soul into helping the Council for National Parks. They are heroes and heroines of the first order.

If I didn't get to the Dales regularly I would start to shrink as a human being. My soul is still happiest at Malham Tarn. The lake is always clear, the clouds are overhead and there is peace. Malham Cove and Gordale Scar give me images of dinosaurs. They are wonderfully primitive places, especially after heavy rain.

The Yorkshire Dales is the centre of the earth. That is why I commend this special celebration of the area and its people.

Favourite Places

"Wharfedale, where I was born and brought up, will always be my favourite dale. We went to a part of it every weekend when I was little - Bolton Abbey or Barden Tower, Burnsall or Grassington. One of my favourite photographs is of me standing with our two dogs - Grace and Favour, now no longer with us - at Bolton Abbey. Happy days!"

Alan Titchmarsh

(Photo: Michael J Stead)

"One of my early memories of the Yorkshire Dales was when Yorkshire County Cricket Club visited Settle in 1959 to play against them in 1959. I also played for Yorkshire County Cricket that year in another charity match against Pateley Bridge at the annual Nidderdale Show. Once out of the urban sprawl we travelled through some beautiful countryside and pretty villages before reaching the grounds.

"I returned to Settle a number of times to visit and stay with Don Wilson, who lived there and started out playing for the Yorkshire team at the same time as me. I have spent many happy hours with him and on my own visiting the surrounding Dales."

Dickie Bird

Introduction

This book has been written to celebrate the fiftieth anniversary of the Yorkshire Dales becoming a National Park in 1954. It was the seventh Park to be designated, following on from the Lake District, Peak District, Snowdonia, Dartmoor, Pembrokeshire Coast and North York Moors. All were born on a wave of post-war idealism that has never quite been matched in reality. They are different to national parks in other parts of the world in that they are not wilderness areas but have several thousand inhabitants and the land largely remains in private ownership.

The statutory duties of National Park Authorities are to preserve and enhance the natural beauty, wildlife and cultural heritage of the area, and to promote opportunities for the understanding and enjoyment of its special qualities by the public. At the same time they have a duty to foster the economic and social well being of the local communities. It does not take much consideration of these three objectives to realise that conflict is inevitable.

Despite such an obvious recipe for discord, the Yorkshire Dales National Park has overcome a neglected childhood when it was administered by parents who had opposed its creation. These were the North Riding and West Riding County Councils, who appointed a permanent staff of just two. Matters improved steadily from the mid-1970s and today the Park has over a hundred full-time employees and an annual budget of £4.76 million. Its committed staff safeguard an area of astonishing variety, forming some of the finest countryside in Britain and now attracting around eight million visitors a year.

The following pages have been devised at several levels. The photographs and paintings form a visual celebration of a landscape and its people, and strive to capture qualities that speak to the spirit so powerfully as sometimes to defy adequate description. The text goes behind the scenery, reflecting on fifty years of change and focusing on the problems as well as the pluses of rural living. Special emphasis is placed on local people, as there has been belated recognition that without their support the National Park as currently known and loved will soon cease to exist. Finally, and unusually for a book, children at Primary School convey in prose, poems, paintings and drawings the things that they like most –and least! – about living in the Dales. Their thoughts certainly give cause for reflection.

Although published in association with the Yorkshire Dales National Park Authority, the views expressed in this book are those of the author and not the Authority, its members or its officers. That said, I have tried to avoid personal opinion and instead present an objective picture, which means that in some areas it is easier to celebrate yesterday than today. The main exception is the final section, "Looking Ahead", which inevitably takes the form of crystal ball gazing and is therefore subjective.

Many people have helped me to bring to fruition what at times has seemed an impossible task, namely completing a book that five months ago was little more than an idea. Colin Speakman eased the burden by agreeing to write the chapters "Travelling around the Dales" and "Enjoying the Yorkshire Dales". Ruth Campbell succeeded brilliantly in getting three generations of a Coverdale farming family together to tell in their own words how their world has changed. I count it a great privilege again to have had the support of Marie Hartley, born in 1905 and now occupying a unique place as the most senior of all social historians of the Dales. Ann Holubecki's recollections and photographs of farming in Wensleydale in the 1960s have been especially helpful. I am also very grateful to award-winning novelist Jane Gardam for taking time out from a busy schedule to write about her beloved Swaledale.

Elizabeth Metcalfe approached a number of personalities for their support, with the resulting contributions from David Bellamy, Alan Titchmarsh and Dickie Bird. Further input has come from David Hockney and Brian Blessed. The co-ordinator of the National Park's fiftieth anniversary celebrations, Cathy Bennett, has shown infectious enthusiasm for this book from the outset and has always cheerily answered what must now be hundreds of e-mails. John Sayer kindly read the chapters relating to farming and tactfully pointed me in the right

The Yorkshire Dales at its finest. The hamlet of Halton Gill, where most of the houses are over three hundred years old. New building, as instanced by the barns in the right foreground, has been carefully designed to harmonise with the landscape. Beyond stretches Littondale, its U-shape clearly showing its glacial origins. The dry stone walls criss-crossing the valley floor set the Dales apart from almost anywhere else in the world. (Colin Raw)

direction. Artists and photographers have promptly responded to my appeals and I am sorry that I have been able to include only a fraction of the images submitted. Teachers at Primary Schools have cajoled some five hundred pieces of work from what appear to have been willing pupils - and made the final selection of just fifty submissions extremely difficult.

Despite the hundreds of books already published on the Yorkshire Dales, I hope it doesn't sound too presumptuous to say that this one is different. I trust it forms a unique anniversary celebration of some of the world's most glorious landscape and wonderful people.

David Joy
Holebottom Farm, Hebden,
Yorkshire Dales

March 2004

Part 1

Fifty Years Ago

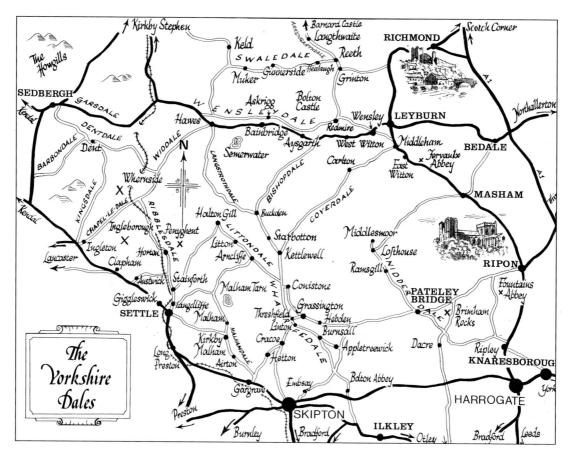

Map of the Yorkshire Dales showing the surrounding area and centres of population. It includes Nidderdale, which was excluded from the National Park, reputedly because Bradford Corporation did not want visitors trampling over the gathering grounds for its reservoirs at the valley head.

The Quiet Dales

One December morning in the mid-1950s a distinguished group assembled at the Red Lion Hotel in Burnsall. There were no less than four aldermen and three justices of the peace, all members of the Yorkshire Electricity Board. After pleasantries they piled onto a coach and headed up to Litton, no doubt already looking forward to a sumptuous lunch back at the Red Lion. But first there was the important business of the day, the grandly titled "Switching on Ceremony of the Littondale Section of the Upper Wharfedale Electrification Scheme".

It was one of many such events taking place as power lines marched up the Dales, bringing transformation in their wake. Villages had for some time been receiving electricity from generating plants or hydroelectric schemes, but these often struggled and in many households it was not uncommon for the lights to go out if the iron was switched on!

Then suddenly, at the click of a switch, there was mains electricity - and light! Homesteads were quick to install electric cookers, washing machines and, above all, television sets, which happily had just become generally available at this time. One moment it was grim isolation and the next the whole world was there in glorious black and white. The Tiller Girls high kicked across the screen

and the daily round for the average farmer would never be the same again. There has been no more instant change in the life of Dales people.

This transformation may well have helped to fortify a group of local inhabitants, who in 1954 came out fighting when a quarry company set its sights on Butterhaw, one of the six internationally famous reef knolls that lie between Thorpe and Cracoe in Upper Wharfedale. Weary of the constant dust and noise from neighbouring Swinden Quarry (as graphically shown on page 44 of this book), and fearful of what lorries would do to the narrow road to Thorpe, nearby residents decided that enough was enough. A petition of over a thousand signatures was soon gathered and the Council for the Preservation of Rural England was moved to note: "Many Geologists and Ladies interested in the countryside also registered objections."

The geologists included Dr Arthur Raistrick, doyen of Dales historians, who testified to the "beauty and completeness" of the reef knolls as a group of hills. They formed "a classic ground known to geologists everywhere, including some of the highest ranking Americans". Accusing the company of targeting Butterhaw solely because it would be easy to quarry,

Mains electricity had still to reach much of the Dales in the mid-1950s. Symbolic of this era was the common practice of hand-milking cattle in a dank and gloomy barn, often remote from the main farm. Frank Thackray, perched on a traditional three-legged milking stool, is busy at work at Park House, Bordley. (Marie Hartley)

The designation of the Yorkshire Dales National Park in 1954 caused scarcely a ripple in the area, but there was great concern about the loss of one of its scenic landmarks. Public protest played a key role in defeating proposals to create a limestone quarry at Butterhaw, one of the famous series of "reef knolls" near Thorpe in Wharfedale. This panorama of what was almost lost shows Butterhaw at left with trees at its base. Stebden Hill is at right with a third reef knoll – Elbolton – visible through the gap. (David Joy)

Dr Raistrick concluded: "The existence of the knolls as a continuous group is an essential feature and the removal of any one of them would in no way be compensated by the preservation of the rest."

There are generally two sides to every story - and so it was as Butterhaw. Another distinguished geologist, Dr R G S Hudson, accused the protesters of insincerity and expressed "gratitude to the quarry owners of the West Riding". He explained: "The more quarries they open, the more geological facts are available, and the yet more theories will the geologist propound." Dr Hudson added that he had long hoped another quarry would be established close to Swinden: "Of the various sites likely, when quarried to provide information of scientific value, Butterhaw is the most suitable. It could be completely quarried away without harm."

The protesters eventually won the day but only after

fighting a second proposal to extract limestone from Stebden Hill, another of the reef knolls. The company concerned went into retreat and today these green and rounded hills remain unspoilt.

After this wave of excitement the Dales reverted to its characteristic slumbers of the 1950s, when much of the area was so quiet that the only sounds were the bleating of sheep and the calls of curlew and lapwing. There were no low-flying jets, little traffic and an almost total absence of powered machinery. At night only the occasional hoot of an owl disturbed Wordsworth's "silence that is in the starry sky, the sleep that is among the lonely hills".

Life went on in 1954 unaffected by such national milestones as Roger Bannister's breaking of the four-minute mile, the birth of ITV or even the broadcasting of the eight hundredth episode of "The Archers". Far more excitement was caused locally when Wensleydale farmer Ambrose Harker paid £1,800 - nearly three times the previous record - for a Swaledale ram, And there was much peeping through net curtains when a peculiar contraption resembling a giant vacuum cleaner headed north from Grassington on a large lorry. It turned out that the Inglebys of Nether Heselden were taking delivery of Littondale's first hay blower. Reflecting the spirit of the age is a photograph that shows two members of the family - fully attired in waistcoat and tie - forking hay into the tractor-driven pneumatic tube so that it could be swept straight into the barn.

Farming inevitably featured in an outstanding topographical book *The Yorkshire Dales,* which Marie Hartley and Joan Ingilby were then writing. They noted: "The farms are usually mixed, and small enough to be run by the farmer and his family. It is almost essential to be born in the Dales to succeed on one." On broader issues, MH and JI regretted the continuing depopulation of the more remote valleys but concluded: "What strikes us is the neatness, cleanliness and extreme quiet of the villages of the Dales. Yet in spite of depletion in numbers they are lively and have resources for most needs."

The inspiration for the book was an idea that had been talked about for more than twenty years. It may have been a case of hope deferred making the heart sick, but certainly there was no formal celebration and little fuss when the 680 square mile Yorkshire Dales National Park formally came into being in October 1954. Having opposed its creation, the North Riding and West Riding County Councils took the "Yes Minister" approach of setting up a joint advisory committee, which after due prodding finally held its first meeting in April 1957. It was a masterpiece of procrastination.

One of the landmark books of the last fifty years has been "The Yorkshire Dales" by Marie Hartley & Joan Ingilby, published in 1956 and still an excellent introduction to the area. The two authors were photographed in their Askrigg studio by Bertram Unné, an outstanding photographer of the period whose work is featured elsewhere in this book. Happily, his negatives were acquired by North Yorkshire County Council and many of the images are now on the Internet (www.northyorks.gov.uk/unnetie).

Portrait of the 1950s

A boundary sign provides a clear reminder that the Yorkshire Dales National Park was originally divided between the North Riding and West Riding County Councils, who were in fact the chief opponents to its creation. Signs such as this one at the head of Wensleydale were swept away following local government reorganisation in 1974. The Moorcock Inn forms the centrepiece of this car-free scene.

Many postal deliveries in the 1950s were still on foot, with wellington boots essential wear for much of the year. But there was always time for a chat, as seen here at Thoralby in Bishopdale.

Although the Ferguson tractor and the Land Rover were making inroads, the age of the quad bike was far in the future and horses still played a vital role on many farms.

(Above) Hay is wrapped round the horse as a means of taking it to feed sheep in outlying fields – a practice known as "jagging". The farmer is Brian Fawcett of Greenses, near Keld in Swaledale.

(Left) Another scene at Greenses, with Francis and Brian Fawcett muck-spreading by hand from a low cart.
(Marie Hartley - 2)

(Top)   *Lime dressing in lower Wensleydale, in the days when this was a regular event on many pastures.*

(Right)   *Bracken was once cut as bedding for stock, a practice that also helped keep the fells clear of this noxious plant that has spread alarmingly in recent years. Horses and sleds – an age-old means of transport – are being used to bring large quantities of bracken down to Riddings, a farm on the western edge of the National Park at Howgill, near Sedbergh.*

Branch lines still served Dales communities such as Grassington, Hawes and Richmond in the 1950s, although their days were numbered. They conveyed all manner of freight – including cattle, here being herded onto a train in May 1955 under the watchful eye of the Station Master.

When vastly more farms were in milk, another symbol of the age at the end of many a lane was a wooden platform. On it would be perched milk kits waiting collection by the lorry from the dairy.

Although taken just outside the Dales, this picture is representative of many a home interior during this period. Matting rather than carpets cover what would probably be a flagged floor, so the farmer has come straight off the fields still wearing his boots. The old black-leaded range has a modern replacement, in front of which the kids play with their Dinky toys on a peg rug. A radio powered by large acid batteries provides a link with the outside world.

Just surviving into the 1950s was the long tradition of hand-knitting in the Dales. Martha Dinsdale, one of the last exponents of the craft, is seen at Appersett in Wensleydale with her family and a gaggle of geese. The rearing and selling of geese then commonly provided an additional source of farm income – especially for women. (Bertram Unné)

Peat cutting was another activity that lingered into the 1950s. Like so many chores of those days, it was unremitting toil and involved not just digging the peat but stacking, drying and getting the turves down from the moor. Cherry and Isabella Kearton are working with their daughter Martha at peat diggings in remote Stock Dale west of Thwaite. (Marie Hartley)

Hiring days also petered out in the 1950s. Only a relatively few men have gathered in Hawes on what would be one of the first two market days in July. Those seeking employment – often Irishmen – bargained with local farmers needing help during haytime. (Lucie Hinson collection)

Tools of the times – 1. A cross-cut saw being used in the correct way, as close to the ground as possible, to fell a tree that has already had its base shaved with an axe.

Tools of the times – 2. Scythes were still used to do jobs that today would be tackled more quickly – and more noisily – by powered hover mowers and strimmers. A roadside bank near Keld is here being shorn in the time-honoured manner.

A close-knit family group at Bell Busk, near Gargrave. The children are wonderfully posed by W Hubert Foster, an official railway photographer who took many superb pictures of the Settle to Carlisle line but also portrayed local life with equal skill.

Many Dales children lived an isolated existence in the 1950s, so even relatively humdrum events such as the weekly visit of the travelling grocer assumed special significance. In this scene, three eager youngsters are about to "help" mum collect provisions from "Swaledale's Original Mobile Stores".

Village sports were often the highlight of the year. Although the tradition still continues in the Dales, fewer such events still retain their fancy dress parade. This group had assembled on Askrigg Sports Day in the early 1950s to put on a display that was both inventive and topical. (Marie Hartley)

Grouse beating has long been a useful source of income for Dales youngsters in the summer holidays. A local lad is here taking a lunchtime break with Thomas Joy, the last shepherd of Grassington Moor.

Once they had left school the majority of Dales children found employment on the land. A young member of the Lambert family at Mile House, Conistone, clearly has his heart set on working with sheepdogs. (Bertram Unné)

A major difference between then and now was that most winters were much colder, with plenty of frost and snow rather than muggy rain. Sometimes conditions would be sufficiently harsh for rivers and lakes to freeze over, as here at Malham Tarn on a sunny but bitterly cold January day.

Part 2

The Changing Dales

Despite what the pessimists might say, change in the Yorkshire Dales over the last half century has often been for the better rather than the worst. The value of nature conservation has received greater recognition – a trend celebrated by Wensleydale artist Judith Bromley in her books "Step into the Meadow" and "Come Down to the Wood". Her painting of the stile leading to the meadow captures the richness of the flora that happily flourishes.

Fifty Years of Change

There is a favourite place high above Upper Wharfedale. The view extends northwards in a vast sweep across rolling moor and outcrops of millstone grit to the majestic bulk of Great Whernside. Westwards the grey rock gives way to glistening white limestone and the River Wharfe snaking serpent-like down its glacier-scarred valley. To the south are the extraordinary reef knolls around Thorpe, faintly reminiscent of sleeping elephants.

Threatening clouds are scudding across the sky with occasional bursts of rain coming almost horizontally on the wind. The dale below has an eggshell finish in the flat light, but then suddenly a window opens in the grey mass overhead and sunshine bursts forth. Momentarily, the colours switch from dull green to brilliant emerald, from gloomy brown to gold and copper, but seconds later the dazzling display is over as quickly as it began.

Less than a couple of miles away as the curlew flies, crowds will be thronging Burnsall's riverside and Grassington's cobbled square, but away to the north it is quite possible to walk over empty acres for more than half a day without meeting a living soul. The only encounters are likely to be with sheep grazing on moorland once dismissed by a Dales farmer as "nowt but scenery".

Although written today, these words could equally well have been penned fifty years ago. In some ways the title of this chapter is a misnomer, for the all-important factor about the Dales is not how much has changed but how little. Evolution has generally triumphed over revolution and, for reasons explained more fully in the next chapter, the basic landscape has so far largely avoided ruination by modern development.

The intricate patchwork of dry stone walls still transform what would otherwise be a fairly bleak and certainly less interesting scene. Dating back to medieval times, they were built without the aid of modern transport, machinery and tools on a scale that is almost beyond comprehension. Thanks to various grant schemes, voluntary labour and financial input from the Yorkshire Dales Millennium Trust, the walls are in better shape than has been the case for many a year.

They provide a haven for flowers growing alongside paths and field edges such as foxgloves on the more acid sandstone or the dazzling displays of meadow cranesbill and scabious on the limestone. The Dales has retained its flora better than most places in England as is also the case with its wildlife in general. Native roe deer can still be found by the stealthy and patient, while badgers are

The characteristic dry stone walls of the Dales, which once seemed likely to slip into terminal decline, have now had their worth fully recognised and a huge repair programme has been put in hand. This painting, also by Judith Bromley, shows that the walls can often be at their best in damp weather when the lichens and mosses glisten like jewels on the grey stones.

It is the stone walls that single out these two photographs and mean that such scenes could arguably be taken nowhere else in the world. Some of the more ancient field boundaries have outlived their usefulness as instanced on Elbolton, looking towards Grassington (left – Colin Raw), but the general panorama is still a wonderful patchwork. It shows at its absolute finest as the afternoon sun highlights the fields around Gunnerside in Swaledale (above – Mike Kipling Photography)

Major landscape changes in the Dales have been less than in many National Parks, with coniferous afforestation and limestone quarrying both attracting increasing opposition. On the other hand, the massive expansion of Grimwith Reservoir in the 1970s caused little protest – perhaps because of its sheer remoteness close to the watershed of Wharfedale and Nidderdale. This now huge stretch of water was painted on a day of hazy sunlight by Chris Wade.

present but seldom seen. Considerable success has been achieved in bringing back the otter to Dales rivers, notably the Ure and its tributaries. In the skies, many birds of prey are seen in greater numbers, thanks largely to the banning of the more extreme agricultural pesticides that caused a build up of fatal residues from their prey.

Green but not pleasant

The need to provide a refuge for endangered species was one of the reasons put forward in the 1970s to justify the blanket planting of large areas of the Dales with serried ranks of Sitka spruce trees. Quoting the old song "I think that I shall never see a poem lovelier than a tree", forestry interests also argued that the conifers would bring a welcome touch of greenery to the bleak and barren uplands. As explained in the next chapter, the villain of the piece was the short-lived Northern Pennines Rural Development Board, which granted a series of planting licences as an early form of agricultural diversification.

By far the most controversial of the schemes it authorised was at the head of Langstrothdale. J B Priestley was among those who protested, arguing in a letter to *The*

Times that the trees would "destroy the stark magnificence" of this area - "one of our noblest landscapes". Despite this heavyweight opposition, the planting went ahead and the Rural Development Board's demise by no means brought an end to afforestation. Controversy flared up again in 1978 with proposals to plant 300 acres of South House Moor, on the eastern flanks of Ingleborough. To some it was akin to desecration of a sacred mountain. Ultimately the government refused to sanction the necessary grant-aid and the scheme faded away, but this did not stop the foresters setting their sights on Cam Fell in the late 1980s.

This time the dark green tide finally turned. At the heart of much of the criticism was the stark irony that planning committees could determine the size of a house window but were powerless to prevent plantations of several thousand acres simply because they were seen as primarily an agricultural operation exempt from planning control. It became apparent that tree planting was nothing more than a tax loophole for the super rich, a national newspaper naming some of the beneficiaries - including two "former leading lights of the government's

Cattle may no longer be driven through the centre of Hawes on their way to the auction mart (above – Bertram Unné), *but otherwise the highest market town in the Dales is little changed. Labour-saving developments include a launderette with outdoor seats on which to enjoy the sun while the clothes are washed.* (left – John Potter)

Nature Conservancy Council"! Such revelations were swiftly followed by the cessation of tax relief on forestry schemes, with increased planting grants instead being given for broad-leaved woodland. It was the start of new era for tree cover in the Dales with much ancient woodland being restored and many new mixed plantings being made under the protection of the National Park, the Forestry Commission and such bodies as the Woodland Trust and the Yorkshire Dales Millennium Trust.

Stone from the Dales

Limestone has long been taken out of the Dales. It began in the smallest of ways to improve the land and grew into an extractive industry with the coming of the railways. The 1954 "Battle of Butterhaw", described in the last chapter, was the first outward sign that there were limits as to how far the quarry companies could go. Nevertheless, they continued to get virtually everything they wanted from existing quarries and the result was not a pretty sight.

One of the classic Dales views – Burnsall from the fell looking north in the 1950s (Right) *and today* (above – Colin Raw). *Here too changes are not immediately obvious, with new buildings blending well with their surroundings. The most noticeable difference is that the woodland behind the village in the earlier picture has now largely gone, although the wheel will ultimately come full circle through recent re-planting.*

(Above) *This sylvan scene on the green at Arncliffe may suggest a rural idyll, but running through the fabric of village life in the Dales is an emotive and seemingly intractable problem, with the remorseless increase in prices driving most houses out of reach of young people. As a result there is an ageing population.* (Colin Raw)

(Left) *Modern agriculture means that the old-style barn has lost its original purpose – and large numbers have been converted into houses. This early example of such a conversion is at Feizor, near Settle.*

Admitting that it was an emotive reaction provoked by the squalor on the ground, the Craven Branch of CPRE summarised the situation in 1972: "Swinden daily grows more monstrous, forming a blot on the landscape which can be seen for miles. Dust from the quarry is spreading like a creeping white blanket, bringing ugliness to an ever-increasing area of Wharfedale. Eight-wheeled lorries pour out from the works, carrying the tide of depression still further. Elsewhere, the pattern is much the same. Horton quarry has effectively blighted a large area of upper Ribblesdale, while Giggleswick quarry is about to take another bite out of the unique Scar. Even more deplorable is Skirwith quarry in Chapel-le-Dale, totally ruining the entrance to a valley which is without parallel in England. Such desecration makes a mockery of the whole concept of National Parks."

The view of the then West Riding County Council was that it had to balance the unique environment of the Park with the need to assure the continuing supply of necessary materials for industry. Although Swinden quarry commendably switched much of its output from road to rail, the feeling persisted that the Park was decidedly coming off worst in the supposed balancing act. In 1986 there was great concern when the life of Coolscar quarry, immediately behind the famous Kilnsey

Crag, was extended for a further ten years. Four years later an independent survey showed that a lorry from the Ribblesdale quarries was passing through Settle roughly every ninety seconds, making a total of over 500 vehicle movements per day. Adding to the public anger was the fact that much of the high-grade limestone was being squandered as aggregates for new road schemes.

A major concern was the number of dormant planning consents, some going back to the early 1950s and including a 24-hectare site in the heart of the Three Peaks district at Ribblehead. Yet in a similar way to afforestation, the climate of public opinion was now changing and in 1998 the quarry industry announced that it would not, in the normal course of events, be applying for any new workings in National Parks. Later the same year the Ribblehead consent was voluntarily surrendered without any request for compensation, the company stating that it would be "irresponsible" to retain its rights to quarry on the flanks of Ingleborough.

It was a defining moment - and one that would have seemed unthinkable two decades earlier. It was in effect a negotiated settlement as succinctly pointed out by the *Craven Herald*: "This heralds the end of quarrying in the Dales. But it will be a phased withdrawal rather than a

Two ages meet at Keld in Swaledale. A new house has a load of manure for its garden delivered by horse and cart. (Bertram Unné)

Scargill Chapel, Upper Wharfedale, designed by the distinguished church architect George Pace who wanted it "to appear to grow out of the ground". On completion in 1961, it was widely acclaimed for its "sympathetic affinity with local traditional building, while achieving a strikingly modern effect". Critics of today's planning system feel that policy is strangling imagination and fear that inspirational architecture in the Dales will henceforth be conspicuous by its absence. (Geoff Lund)

scorched earth retreat leaving the ugly scars of battle."

Nowhere to live!

While the key issues of afforestation and quarrying have to a large extent been resolved, the same unfortunately cannot be said of ongoing problems over housing. These have often become highly emotive, embracing the plight of young people wanting to live in the Dales but prevented from doing so by high prices. At times the arguments have assumed a level of vitriol that has no place in a celebratory book, but the issues have to be faced fair and square as they lie at the heart of the area's present and future well-being.

By the mid-1980s it was clear that long-established problems on the housing front were not only worsening but doing so at an accelerating rate. The mere fact of National Park status ironically meant that people were prepared to give anything to live in the area - and did so. House prices continued to rise ahead of the national average as dwellings were bought by affluent incomers, often as retirement or holiday homes. Many villages already had more than half their houses empty through the winter months. Smaller and cheaper accommodation virtually ceased to exist, which meant that young people unable to find a home were leaving the area with a consequent knock-on effect on schools, shops and transport.

In 1985 the Yorkshire Rural Community Council carried out a groundbreaking survey of the housing situation in Wensleydale. It raised real fears of an ageing population, lacking the traditional social mix of Dales life, with the area destined to become a northern "Costa Geriatrica" for the elderly and privileged. The survey put forward a number of key recommendations, most of them aimed directly at local people. They included more flexible planning policies to meet local needs, grants to enable locals to buy houses - with restrictions on resale, and a raft of better advice and information. There was also support for Housing Association schemes, whereby

Village shops in the Dales are in decline due in some cases to a reduced resident population but also to the advent of supermarkets and even Internet shopping. The village shop-cum-post office at Thoralby in Bishopdale has a large variety of items on view, with other goods stored in drawers behind the counter ready to be weighed out on the brass scales.

voluntary bodies are eligible to obtain government funding through the Housing Corporation to build new homes. None of the recommendations was controversial but all required a degree of commitment and political will that had hitherto been lacking. Almost twenty years later, few have been implemented.

Instead, the problems have assumed centre stage as the media has increasingly focussed on such issues as rural poverty and deprivation. The consequences of the lack of affordable housing have also become more evident. The 2001 census revealed a remarkable 6.2 per cent increase in the number of people living in the National Park, which now stands at 19,654. Yet more than a fifth are aged over 65 and there are strong indications that the inward migration from the older end of the age spectrum is not replacing the outward migration of young people. A survey in 2003 of primary schools at Hawes, Bainbridge, Askrigg and West Burton found that the proportion of local children - defined as those whose grandparents live in Wensleydale - was falling sharply and that the drop was not being compensated for by children whose

families were moving into the area.

Similarly, there is also a shortage of housing for manual workers. By 2003 many local businesses were finding it difficult if not impossible to recruit staff. The Wensleydale Creamery at Hawes hit the headlines when in the run-up to Christmas it had to employ thirty Indian workers supplied by a Birmingham agency. Its managing director, David Hartley, commented bluntly: "There is no longer a rural pool of labour available to carry out these jobs at peak periods. People talk about regeneration of the Dales. The employment opportunities are there but people cannot take advantage because of the high cost of housing."

Bald statistics scarcely convey the true scale of the problem. Average house prices in the Dales passed the £200,000 mark in 2002, whereas incomes are less than two-thirds the national average. A survey in Ingleton revealed 125 families with a housing need that could not be satisfied, most of them putting the maximum mortgage they could afford at £85,000 - not enough to

Sports and games in the Dales have always been of the homespun kind, which may be why so many have survived as they undoubtedly have traditional appeal.

(Above) *Wallops being played in the middle of the street at Redmire Feast in 1967. The game is similar to skittles except that sticks are thrown instead of balls.*

(Left) *Trotting races remain popular at several Dales shows. Many of the horses at Hawes Sports in 1966 were pacers, whose gait moves the near-side legs forward together and similarly the off-side legs.* (Marie Hartley – 2)

The many clear rivers and becks mean that fishing is arguably the most popular sport in the Dales with re-stocking always given due importance. In 1965 a lorry had delivered yearling trout to the Rose & Crown at Bainbridge (left). Redvers Hopper and his granddaughter Jemima then used a milk kit to transfer the fish to the river at nearby Yorescott, where the farm has fishing rights along a stretch of the Ure (right). (Ann Holubecki – 2)

buy even a basic two-bedroom starter home. At the other end of the spectrum, it was estimated that an absentee homeowner could earn more in twenty weeks through renting out his property as a holiday cottage than a hill farmer could make in a year.

Caught somewhere between a rock and a hard place in finding a way forward is the Yorkshire Dales National Park Authority. All too often its primary purposes are in conflict, as demonstrated in 2002 when massive media coverage highlighted the plight of Sharon Spensley and her partner James Winspear, a Dales builder and waller, and their young family. National and local planning policies led their proposal for conversion of an isolated barn into a permanent home to be turned down, but what really fanned the flames was the contention that its use as a holiday cottage would have been allowed on the grounds of farm diversification.

The resulting furore at least prompted a fresh look at existing policies, with an ongoing debate on how more could be done to provide affordable housing for local people. It also led to renewed calls for the relaxation of planning controls, as typified by one estate agent who commented: "It's wrong to preserve the Dales in aspic, it's a living environment." Similar sentiments were expressed in a broader context by the Country Land and Business Association (CLA), which early in 2004 cited over-restrictive planning rules as a prime reason for Britain's housing crisis. Its report Housing and the Rural Economy received high praise, but anyone expecting a quick fix should bear in mind that several of the key recommendations are depressingly similar to those in the Yorkshire Rural Community Council's survey way back in 1985.

Tingle factors
Lack of progress on the housing front is no reason for total despondency. As suggested in the concluding chapter of this book, there is much that can be done to solve the present problems without putting at risk the natural beauty, wildlife and cultural heritage that originally led to the Yorkshire Dales being designated a National Park. Thanks first to James Herriot and more recently to the Calendar Girls, its scenery and character is now famous throughout the world.

(Above) *Although some will argue that quarrying activities have no place in a National Park, there can be no doubt that many aspects of the large Swinden Quarry in Upper Wharfedale have greatly improved since this photograph was taken in the early 1950s. The main road then ran through the middle of the plant, which spewed out smoke and lime dust over a wide area. Today the road has been diverted, the quarry plant is partially screened by trees and much of the output is taken away by rail, thereby reducing the amount of lorry traffic.*

(Opposite) *Lead miners did not have to contend with National Park considerations as their industry ended some 120 years ago. In health terms the pollution from a lead smelting mill was infinitely more hazardous than any limestone quarry at its worst, but time heals and many of the remains are now preserved as important historical artefacts. The flues leading up to the smelt-mill chimney on Grassington Moor, here painted by Hannah Chesterman, form part of a large area that has been scheduled by English Heritage as an Ancient Monument.*

This writer occasionally becomes complacent about his surroundings, but it only needs a trip over the "High Road" from Airton to Settle to put matters back in perspective. The last few magic miles can provide one of the great tingle factors of the Dales. On a cold and clear morning, sheep are highlighted by the low sun and cattle in thick winter coats form a perfect foreground to Attermire Scars, the jagged cliffs of glistening white limestone so closely resembling a miniature version of the Dolomites. Ingleborough, blanketed in snow, stands out like a beacon on the far side of Ribblesdale. On one recent occasion it was possible to stop and chat to a Dales farmer in search of some missing ewes. He was definitely one of your native dalesmen - forthright but the absolute salt-of-the-earth. The encounter was a reminder that, although there has been change in the Dales during the last fifty years, the things that really matter still for the moment endure.

At Home in Swaledale

Jane Gardam has had a home near Gunnerside for over twenty years, where she has written many of her award-winning novels and short stories.

I first saw Swaledale in 1928 at Christmas-time when I was five months old and lying in a basket on the back seat of my parents' Austin 7. We were travelling from my home in Redcar to my grandparents' farm in Cumberland. I can't say I remember the journey which was apparently rather hectic as my father had just learned to drive – there was no test then – and was terrified of the (very occasional) oncoming traffic. When another car hove in sight he would stand on the brake and close his eyes. I believe we left the car – our first and last – in Cumberland and returned by train via Newcastle.

Swaledale is the dale that didn't have the railway, though there were plans that finally fizzled out. It has never been a great place for public transport and a random bus is still greeted rapturously, like a lifeboat. I was therefore sixteen before I saw the dale again, this time from my bike youth-hostelling from Redcar to tiny Viking Keld at the top of the upper dale. It was in the middle of World War II and two schoolfriends and I took two days over the journey, stopping the first night in the lower dale at

Grinton, the bottle-neck of the dale which upper dale people used to boast they'd never been beyond. Only last year I heard of an old Keld lady who said she'd only once been further than Grinton when her daughter took her to Darlington to buy a hat.

I don't remember Grinton in 1944. I don't remember the wonderful low-slung church or the even older house beside it, where medieval monks kept a Christian presence, making forays up the dale to try and interest the upper dale in Christianity. They were often driven back down again.

Swaledale then was covered by the great Swaledale Forest and remnants of it survive in Rowleth Woods, between Gunnerside and Low Row. I know them well, for I sit looking at them for hours from the upstairs living-room of our house high above the river. The trees have an ancient, hazy look like an old person's greying but still curly hair. There is a so-called path through them with a National Park signpost, but the dale is so steep here and the trees so tight together that walkers tend to fall out of the eastern end of the wood in a state of collapse.

I remember my bike-ride from Grinton to Keld very well for it was all I could do to keep pedalling. My friends were big strong lasses – one of them became a champion cyclist – and I was small then, and bookish. My bike was a sit-up-and-beg and theirs were racing models. I had never seen such a steep and winding road.

Yet I do remember the snaking silver river, the water-meadows shining bright green, the stone field-houses in the middle of the fields, the few and silent people, the old men sitting on seats in the villages balancing their chins on the tops of their walking-sticks and the fields full of peaceful sheep all much the same today.

Jane Gardam, photographed in Swaledale.

The view is almost too beautiful – Swaledale looking up the valley from opposite Low Row. In the middle of the picture, slightly right of centre, is Rowleth Woods. The trees have "an ancient, hazy look like an old person's greying but still curly hair".

(Geoff Lund)

I next saw Swaledale when I was twenty-eight and we had stopped the car up near the river's source, on the Bronze Age road from Kirkby Stephen. We had come from home in London via the Lake District and now were repeating or reversing history by taking our first child to Redcar to meet his grandparents. When we got out of the car the wind nearly knocked us all down and the baby shouted and laughed. The grass on the fells above the young river in the peaty cleft below us was long and gold. I said, "We could live here".

But I was middle-aged before I came back. I had perforce to live in the south, but I had been writing about the north for some years and all of us every year came for holidays. Then one day I met Elizabeth Gunn who had just published her book on Dorothy Wordsworth and she asked me to her house in the upper dale, on Whitaside. I coveted it instantly, a strange old place surrounded by sinister trees and a front door with an oak bar, put there

against the Scots. Mrs. Gunn had written a lovely novel, *The Rainbow Comes and Goes* which it does up there and had no plans to move, but "That one is up for sale", she said, and pointed. Far away below stood a midget of a house with a barn and two acres, and there we have been for twenty-two years.

The view is almost too beautiful. "You'll never do any work", said my friend, the children's writer, William Mayne, "looking at that ridiculous great back-drop". But we risked it. I work in the barn looking south into the side of a field and watched only by sheep.

From the house we mostly watch the Swale, the fastest flowing river in England that can burst its banks one morning and shrink to a thread the next. Mist rises from the river on summer mornings and rainbows don't only come and go but have the Dales' distinction of sometimes turning themselves upside down. In May they appear to the accompaniment of cuckoos calling over the fields of wild flowers.

Since the farmers have been induced to cut hay later, the wild flowers have spread wonderfully and you don't see tourists digging up primroses in our lane any more. Since the once-despised incomers have arrived and settled the old farmhouses, gardens have changed. Sometimes there are horrors: migraine colours and suburban shrubs and it is difficult to find a real cottage garden anymore, but there is much loving care and the climate-change gives us roses and apple trees where once we'd never have dreamed of trying them.

But Swaledale is not now, and has never been, an earthly paradise. When the leadmines failed people starved or emigrated. There are dozens of sad old mine shafts. Lately, though the farmers were brilliantly successful in avoiding Foot and Mouth as the pyres burned in the Dales around them, sheep-farming is at rock-bottom and the price offered for milk is insulting. There are only two dairy herds left in the upper dale now. "We can't live on beauty", said a farmer's son. "If we could life would be a doddle".

And there is crime. We have been burgled three times, the last time losing everything but the beds. Now our times in the house are pretty spartan. All about the dale we hear of fly-by-night thieves who take farm vehicles from before the farmers' eyes. Mobile phones don't work yet in the Dale and the nearest policeman is usually miles away.

Preserved hay meadow near Muker. Since the farmers have been induced to cut hay later, the wild flowers have spread wonderfully. (Colin Raw)

The fields full of peaceful sheep. Low Row and Feetham from the south side of Swaledale. (Geoff Lund)

It is becoming likely that we shall move away. We are old and the journey from the south gets worse. My publisher and my children are in London and Dorset. Time to go.

Yet the minute we're back, the idea of leaving seems ludicrous. We're proud to belong – or partly belong: we've been more fully accepted since I found out that I had a Swaledale great, great grandmother though I'm afraid she was only from the lower dale – to belong to a place that has survived so much economic disaster and been so loved and preserved, especially in the last half century. It is probably more beautiful now than when I saw it first.

© Jane Gardam, 2004

The Farming Scene

"Farming in the Dales has always been hard - and now it has got harder." Such might well be the response of your average farmer asked to sum up his lot, but in truth it is not that simple as there is no such thing as a typical Dales farm. There is a world of difference between the rich pastures of broad and fertile valleys such as Wensleydale and the rough moorland of the higher dale heads.

Taking the best bits first, Wensleydale stretching down towards Leyburn and the eastern edge of the National Park has always been famous for milk and cheese. In the 1960s the Hawes creamery, created by the famous dalesman Kit Calvert, was handling 4,500 gallons of milk a day and annually producing over a quarter of a million of its famous one-pound cheeses. Large quantities of milk also passed through the Express Dairy at Leyburn prior to export in bulk to Bradford, Hull and Liverpool.

Many farms combined cattle with sheep, as exemplified by the Willis family of Carperby, noted for their pioneering work with the Wensleydale breed. When Richard Joy, agricultural correspondent of the *Yorkshire Post* and father of the present writer, visited them in 1954 they had a high-quality ram breeding flock founded in 1814 and probably the oldest in the north. At the same time they were running a herd of over a hundred Dairy Shorthorns, painstakingly built up and famous for its high milk yields. John Willis was then the third generation of the family at Manor Farm, the whole enterprise echoing the importance of tradition and continuity.

They and their neighbours lived in a different world. Hours were long and exhausting but farming was done in a natural way according to the rhythm of the seasons with little interference from big business or bureaucracy.

(Above) *Lambing time is one of the great landmarks of the farming year. This classic photograph shows W Calvert of Thorns Farm, near Keld, holding twin lambs in the 1960s.* (Marie Hartley)

(Opposite) *Sheep on common grazing or stinted pastures are periodically rounded up for such occasions as clipping or dipping. This round-up in the early 1960s is taking place above Kettlewell.*

(Right) *The Bowdin family dipping sheep at Hebden in Wharfedale about 1960. Modern dips are designed for more efficient one-man operation.* (David Joy)

Watching sheep being clipped by hand with old-fashioned shears was always an experience that could not fail to impress. If there was a good rise to the fleece, the operation could be completed in less than five minutes.
(Above) *Jim Alderson and John Hall clipping sheep near Beck Meetings at the very head of Swaledale, miles from anywhere but close to the border with what was then Westmorland.* (Marie Hartley)
(Opposite) *The last cut! Handling the shears is H Plews of West Scale Park, above Kettlewell.* (Bertram Unné)

Reputation was everything and there was a genuine community spirit. What was tough in the relative lowlands of Wensleydale was infinitely more demanding higher up the dales. Here the farming scene had changed little in centuries and still revolved round age-old ways, typified by hay-making which involved a horse, mower, hay rakes and lots of toil and sweat in an endeavour to get dry hay into the barn between frequent bouts of rain.

It was all captured in a classic book published in 1968, *Life and Tradition in the Yorkshire Dales* by Marie Hartley and Joan Ingilby. They realised that they were working against the clock, recording practices that stood on the brink of extinction. It took a long time for the tractor to oust the horse on the more remote Dales farms and for machines to replace sweated labour, but once the trend started it gathered pace with extraordinary speed. Farmers will rarely view the past through rose-tinted

spectacles and at the time they perhaps least of all regretted the end of an era. The bracken sledges were simply left to rot by the fell gate!

"Slavery" in the 1970s

Yet it was clear to others that this was a seminal change destined to take what amounted to an independent race of people in its wake. In 1971 the writer and broadcaster Bill Cowley completed a survey of farming in Yorkshire, which ended with poignant words: "The Dales and the dalesmen as they were are already doomed. Perhaps the process was inevitable. The old type Yorkshire dalesman is disappearing fast. Few will be left in another ten years. All that reservoir of wit, character and folk lore will have gone, the blunt independent small farmers, full of dry humour, heroic in mould and poetic in speech, hard working but deeply contented, part of the scenery and of history. Even farming is a rat race now, and only the most

George Robinson (centre) regularly visited Hawes auction mart in 1966 with his travelling van that sold an impressive array of agricultural equipment. What looks to be some quality footwear is prominently displayed. (Marie Hartley)

economically efficient will survive. Some will be dales people, and they will remember their fathers, but they will not be like them."

As part of the survey, Bill Cowley visited Langstrothdale and found that there were still fifteen families above Hubberholme dependent on agriculture. He swiftly concluded that few of them were making a proper living: "What can you say to a young man who is trying to live off 150 acres of limestone shelf with 200 Dalesbred ewes and just two or three suckling cows? He cannot possibly make a minimum agricultural wage."

Another young couple had 400 sheep on 400 acres of similar land - the rent of which was over a £1 an acre - and were trying to boost their income with a dairy herd of 36 cows. But almost all hay had to be bought and there were no buildings for that number of cattle. In winter they had to be kept in half dozens in scattered barns and the milking machine carried around. Bill Cowley summarised the situation in three blunt words: "This is slavery."

It was a similar picture at the head of Swaledale, the most rugged of all the dales and the most essentially dependent on sheep. The low proportion of good bottom-land to fell grazing, shortage of winter keep and

the high cost of transport all aggravated the problem. Some of the more enterprising farmers here were making as much as a Midlands car worker or a London docker but working a twelve to sixteen hour day seven days a week to do so. It was almost a situation of no hope: "The land itself defies modernisation and mechanisation. The Land Rover, the tractor and electricity can help but they cannot here transform an economy."

Perhaps because it was difficult to avoid being pessimistic, these statements received little attention at the time. It is a pity, for they were in many ways prophetic: "The dales are altering fast. Here and there a young couple are setting off bravely to farm in the family tradition against economic odds and ignoring the attraction of civilised amenities, but they are few and far between. In the upper dales their only hope would appear to be in providing accommodation and catering for visitors - and they get little help or encouragement in that from any source."

Bill Cowley pleaded for planning authorities to take a much wider view of social and economic factors and not just look at the landscape. Ideally there should be "strictly regulated" conversion of surplus stone buildings to provide more accommodation and release farm capital,

Hay meadows like this one in Swaledale were once found all over the Dales, but have now largely disappeared thanks to the incentives given to hill farmers to produce cheap food. The result was that fields were sown with alien rye grass, force-fed on fertilisers and cut early for silage. The few old meadows that remain have now achieved almost cult status and many are designated as Sites of Special Scientific Interest. (Granville Harris)

Making hay while the sun shines - using the old ways that lingered on into the 1960s.
(Above) *The Daykin family "strewing" at Newbiggin in Wensleydale. The process involved raking the cut hay into long swathes to assist the drying before it was led from the meadow on a sledge.* (Marie Hartley)
(Opposite, top) *Haytime at Raygill Farm, near Hawes, in 1962 - the last year that the grass was made into foot-cocks. This tiring work involved drawing the hay over a raised foot with a rake before putting a second layer on top that acted as a thatch in poor weather.*
(Lower) *Jemima Hopper and Elizabeth Lambert forming foot-cocks at Raygill with specially shortened hay rakes. These were produced at Askrigg by Ernest "Cloggy" Burton, who with his father once made 12,000 rakes in a single year.* (Ann Holubecki – 2)

but if this was not going to happen then some sort of special National Park subsidy should be paid in compensation. He roundly concluded: "To keep these dales as museum pieces is the one certain way of killing them stone dead. Unless the farms are allowed to cash in on tourism in some way, or realise capital from buildings now agriculturally useless, other strong economic forces already at work will lead to the dales becoming sterilised areas of holiday cottages, afforestation and game preserves."

Swings of the pendulum

The publication of Bill Cowley's findings closely coincided with the brief life and sudden death of the Northern Pennines Rural Development Board, covering the whole of the Yorkshire Dales National Park and also a much larger area stretching right up to the Scottish border. Given sweeping powers to control land purchases and use, the Board sought to encourage farm amalgamations in order to reduce the large number of subsistence holdings where there was "very real hardship".

More controversially, it favoured a policy of taking marginal land out of sheep farming by issuing licences

for large areas of coniferous afforestation. Well over a thousand acres in the Yorkshire Dales were sacrificed to what conservationists saw as serried ranks of blanket tree cover, with areas at the head of Langstrothdale, Raydale and Cotterdale being planted on a scale that was to change them out of all recognition. Such was the outcry that the Board became too much of a political hot potato and was abolished before any good could come of its less radical polices that might have brought new life and hope to the uplands.

Its demise left a question mark over what would happen next, but the answer was not long in coming. Britain joined the European Economic Community in 1973 and money rolled out from Brussels as farmers received huge incentives to grow more and more food, even if it meant damaging the countryside in the process. In the Dales most of the once glorious meadows changed from hay to silage and were fertilised, so that much of the landscape was now an unnatural vivid green in high summer. Fells were overgrazed and dry stone walls replaced by post and wire fences, new buildings constructed and stocking rates increased.

It took a long time for the penny to drop that the system was looking after food production at the expense of looking after farmers and the landscape. Not until 1987 did the government introduce a series of Environmentally Sensitive Areas (ESAs) - an appalling piece of bureaucratic jargon for a praiseworthy concept. The Pennine Dales ESA stretches right up towards the Tyne Valley but at its lower end includes parts of Upper Wharfedale, Langstrothdale, Walden, Dentdale, Swaledale and Arkengarthdale.

The prime reason for the designation was to protect what is described as "the greatest concentration of traditionally-managed meadows and pastures in England". The voluntary scheme commits participants to a five-year period, during which they receive payments for foregoing the right to manage the farm business in the most advantageous way, and in some cases making uneconomic decisions, in the wider public interest.

Use of fertilisers is controlled and hay cannot be cut before 15 July, thus making it impossible to take advantage of earlier spells of dry weather. It is an inflexible system, as instanced by diary records kept over a thirty-year period of the most flower-rich meadows in upper Swaledale. They show that the start of haymaking has varied from June 20th to the end of August! John Sayer, a Littondale farmer closely involved with the inception of the ESA scheme, comments: "The cutting date was advised by environmental 'experts' and has now become accepted, but those of us who have the experience know that the weather does not follow the advice of such people."

Further help has come from the National Park's own Dales Barns and Walls scheme, aimed at keeping at least some of the thousands of redundant barns and the estimated 48,000 miles of walls in repair. Starting in 1990 with a pilot project in upper Swaledale and Arkengarthdale, the eighty per cent grants were justified on the grounds that the alternative was a landscape in ruins.

(This page) *Semerwater in the summer of 1967. It was the last time that hay was taken from the nearby meadow by making large cocks, known as "pikes". These were carefully built to turn water, the sides being combed down with a rake. Baling was introduced the following year.* (Ann Holubecki)
(Opposite, top) *Baling greatly speeded up operations in the hayfield, giving time for a break for "drinkings" at Raygill Farm, near Hawes, in July 1981.* (Ann Holubecki)
(Lower) *The modern way, with grass cut for silage being gathered at the foot of Littondale.* (Colin Raw)

Virtually every meadow had its own barn in the old days – and especially so in Swaledale. It meant that the hay rarely had to be moved any great distance, but forking it off the sledge and into the barn was hard work. Cherry Kearton is about to put another load through the forking hole in this 1967 scene at Moor Close, a remote farm in a tributary valley west of Thwaite. (Marie Hartley)

Downward to disaster

Despite these initiatives the overall trend was a downward drift. In the seven years from 1985 to 1992, hill farmers in Britain saw sheep prices - their main source of income - fall by forty per cent. Farmers in the Dales often found it impossible to sell their farm on retirement, and auction marts, feed suppliers, vets and agricultural contractors all experienced a downturn. Yet the true dalesmen, stoical to the end, still kept their resolve. One of them philosophically commented: "These men up here can dig their toes in and live on nowt, whereas down dale farmers can't. In these hills it's not what you earn. It's what you don't spend."

Such resolve was soon to be tested to the full. By 1999 both cattle and sheep prices had collapsed, with a ewe being sold at Hawes auction mart for a mere 20p. There were various reasons, all utterly outside the control of the immediate area, such as the BSE scare, the end of live lamb exports and a high pound making United Kingdom exports expensive.

Just when it seemed inconceivable that matters could get any worse, Foot and Mouth disease broke out in the early spring of 2001 and quickly plunged the Yorkshire Dales into the worst crisis the area had seen in living memory. It was a nightmare scenario more closely resembling a horror movie. Funeral pyres marked the end of herds of pedigree cattle built up over long years of endeavour, new-born lambs lived for only a few days before being slaughtered and thousands of sheep were culled in ways that often left much to be desired. Farmers became prisoners on their own land, waiting in fear for the first symptoms to appear. The Yorkshire Dales was

(Above) *The Swaledale "barnscape" seen at its finest above Thwaite looking towards Kisdon. Although many of these structures are now redundant, special schemes have been introduced in this area to encourage their preservation as a key part of the overall scene. The sheer number of barns in the Dales prevents such an approach being applied to the National Park as a whole.* (Granville Harris)

(Right) *Modern agriculture demands huge barns which are efficient if not beautiful. Yet careful siting can reduce their impact, as effectively demonstrated at Stockdale Farm above Settle, where some huge structures are almost camouflaged by being sunk deep into the hillside.* (Colin Raw)

(Opposite) *"The Topless Barn", a study by Chris Wade of a once proud building above Kettlewell, evokes the fate of many a similar structure. Where redundant barns are close to a road, the value of the roof slates means that they have often proved a tempting target for thieves.*

(Right) *The interiors of Dales barns are just as fascinating as the outside with oak boskins separating the cow stalls and fodder gangs for holding the hay. Cattle were tied to a ridstake on the side of the boskin. All these features are visible in this drawing by Judith Bromley, which depicts a barn near Askrigg.*

quickly reduced to a no-go area as all footpaths were closed and a ghostly quiet descended on the countryside. Like ripples on a large pond, the effects of the catastrophe spread outwards and embraced the entire economy, reflecting the fact that tourism now provided more employment and earnings in the Dales than farming.

The aftermath lasted into the following year and when it was all over it was clear that life in the area would never be quite the same again. Massive compensation payments meant that farmers whose stock had been culled were initially often better off than those who had escaped the outbreak and were now deprived of anything resembling a market. The result was a lasting legacy of bitterness and deep anger over what was seen as bureaucratic incompetence. In addition there was a sad but inevitable rise in the number of long-established farms being broken up for sale in lots as many took the money and walked away from farming to pastures new.

Recovery - and change

Disasters on this scale can in a strange sort of way often create new hope and a new beginning. So it has proved with Foot and Mouth. In the first instance a Dales Recovery Fund raised £600,000 in just two months, although persuading proud dalesfolk to apply for help from what they perceived as a charity was not easy. In the longer term there was a clear determination to make a clean sweep and consider ideas that had hitherto been rejected.

The outbreak occurred at a time when organic farming had captured the public imagination, with demand for herbicide and pesticide free food far exceeding supply.

There was a feeling abroad that supermarkets were making vast profits at the expense of farmers who by comparison received next to nothing. What better than a venture that fostered the selling of local produce direct to local consumers and visitors, with guarantees of quality and the highest standards of animal welfare? The result was the appearance in local butchers of clearly branded Dales Lamb, which not only proved popular with shoppers but was also quickly put on the menu in several of the area's restaurants. Farmers' markets have been slow in coming to the Dales compared with other parts of Yorkshire, although a number of farms quickly established small shops or web sites for selling direct to the public.

Elsewhere, eyes were cast in the direction of Europe and in particular the more mountainous parts of Austria and Switzerland. Here it is almost the norm for the actual farming to be just one source of income on the farm, with tourism and related enterprises providing a substantial slice of the total earnings. Back at home it is not surprising that the buzzword was diversification, although into what was not always immediately apparent. Some farms simply do not lend themselves to visitor facilities and the demand for farmhouse accommodation is far from infinite.

Nevertheless, there have been many cases of considerable enterprise. One such is Lower Winskill, a hill farm dramatically sited on the eastern flank of Ribblesdale above Langcliffe. Losing all its livestock in the Foot and Mouth outbreak, it has pursued a policy of re-stocking but the main thrust has been the development of a Visitor Centre. Farm buildings have been converted

Once the hay was safely gathered in there was time to relax and also enjoy the annual show, which was – and is – a feature of almost every major dale. Upper Wharfedale Show, held at Kilnsey on the Summer Bank Holiday Tuesday, is now a massive affair but it was not always so. These three earliest known colour photographs of the show date from either 1953 or '54 and depict a much more modest and less commercial event.

(Above) A photograph of today's show could not be taken from the same point as the whole of the foreground is now covered in marquees and tents.

(Opposite, top) Serious business – the Swaledale sheep are judged.

(Lower) Barely a soul is in sight on the field as contestants in the dry stone walling competition go about their task. (Ken Ellwood - 3)

into teaching, display and activity areas with a small residential facility. Visitors are involved in the maintenance of a traditional hay meadow as well as the adjacent limestone pavement and other archaeological features on the farm. Tom Lord, the farmer and now proprietor of the Centre, is a skilled interpreter. The enterprise is also fortunate in boasting several medieval dry stone walls, which provide a key attraction for professionals, students and visitor groups.

Such a venture is miles away from the traditional farm of say twenty years ago but it is surely a sound response to inevitable change. Visitor facilities are being developed without impacting on the countryside and it is the farmer himself who is providing the link between the old era

and the new. This is the key point. There can be no future for the Dales countryside without the skill, care and deep understanding of the Dales farmer. If he goes so too does the irreplaceable mixture of meadows, fell pastures, farmsteads, barns and walls. The issues have long been recognised but solutions have been bedevilled by the lack of a coherent approach among the many parties involved. Farmers and conservationists must now be on the same side as must DEFRA, the National Park Authority and the multitude of other bodies responsible for the area's destiny. Otherwise, a way of life that has endured in the Dales for more than a thousand years will be lost and the area will become a combination of theme park and wilderness.

Three Generations in Coverdale

The Suttill family – Alf, his son Ronnie and grandson David – talk to Ruth Campbell about farming in the dale, reflecting the changes in agriculture and lifestyle over the past fifty years.

Alf Suttill, 87, lives with his wife Annie, 88, in an eighteenth century three-bedroom stone house in the centre of the village of Carlton in Coverdale. Two of their five children are farmers, and five of their ten grandchildren work in farming and agriculture.

I have farmed all my life, I was raised on my auntie's farm at Horsehouses in Coverdale and started working full-time on the farm when I left school at 14. I was up by 6.0am, milking cows and looking after sheep. I was kept busy walling, fencing, hay-making and lambing but it was very different to what we know now. There were no tractors, we had two Dales horses, they did all the work, all the cutting and working of the hay. They dragged an old-fashioned mowing machine for the cutting and a dasher for shaking it around. It was all gathered up with a sweep. We piled it in the barn with pitch forks. We used to lead the manure out with a horse and cart, put it in heaps and spread it. It was hard work, we knew nothing else.

You learnt on the job, as you went along. If you went walling two or three days, you knew how it went, if you trapped your fingers, you wrapped them up in a handkerchief and knew just to keep them out of the way next time, you just carried on. Poor beggars going on courses now and learning how to do dry stone walling, they're wasting their money.

I remember when tractors came about in the forties. They cost a lot of money but were well worth it, they saved a lot of time and made such a difference.

After we married, we rented a farm at Braidley, it was 100 acres with 50 cattle and 100 sheep. I was one of the first to get a tractor in the Dale, there was a lot of interest in it. We got a Bristol first it was on tracks with one wheel at the front.

Then in 1950, with two young sons coming up, we took on the big farm at Coverhead, it was 3,500 acres and we had 1,200 sheep and 80 cattle. It was a lot of work, my wife used to help and we had three or four other people working for us. We were expanding all the time, we became more modern. We got a grey Ferguson petrol tractor, it cost £325 and we still have it now, through it doesn't work. It was money well spent. Two years later we got a second tractor. Things changed tremendously, we had a Land Rover and a car as well, when it went. You had transport, you could go anywhere, you could drive and take stock. We were cutting hay by tractor, they did all the leading and transporting. Everything changed. You didn't have to ride your pushbike anymore. They don't work as hard now, it is easier for them. They ride quad bikes now, they don't know what walking is.

It was a big old stone farmhouse at Coverhead, we had gas lamps and coal fires and an Aga cooker. It was cold but we didn't bother about that, we were there to make a living and feed stock and look after them, that was our main concern. Electricity changed everything. At first, everyone else was getting it and we weren't, nobody took any notice of us, so I wrote to the Prime Minister at Whitehall. I got a reply saying he would do his best and shortly after that electricity came up the dale. We got a TV, my wife and the kiddies loved that. Later, we got central heating at Coverhead, that made a big difference.

I remember some very bad winters, when we got cut off for weeks at a time. The worst was in 1962, there was deep, deep snow, some sheep got overblown. You couldn't get out on the lanes. We used to kill pigs and salt and cure them to get through the winters. There were no fridges or freezers, we had a pantry at the top of the cellar stairs with stone shelves. You had your hens and eggs and our own milk fresh every day. We didn't have tinned food. We would shoot the odd rabbit. We didn't bother much with

Alf Suttill rounding up some of his sheep in the early 1950s.

vegetables. The nearest shop was three or four miles away and I would walk there and bring back the necessaries, sugar and flour, so my wife could bake her bread and things. We would have to do that regularly in winter.

Now the village shop and post office have closed. The shop used to sell everything, groceries of all description, my wife used to get four-stone sacks of flour and sugar for baking, and big bags of currants. We didn't shop anywhere else. It was a lovely shop before and just went down and down. At one time we had a grocery van coming out with biscuits, cakes, pasties and everything, and a bread van. They don't come any more. Different people came into the neighbourhood, shoppers just drifted away to big stores. There are a lot of holiday cottages and only four farms left in the village now. The children went to school in Carlton, a car used to collect them. Now it is closed. A house has been built on the playing fields.

So much has changed. There used to be two churches in Horsehouse, there isn't one now. One is a house, the other is being converted to house. I have seen when they couldn't get into the church, it was well attended on special occasions, got all kinds of preachers. Not many go now, the young ones growing up don't go to church.

We made sure we got our holidays, usually one week in May. We went to Morecambe and Wales, Scotland and Ireland, and when the children got into their teens, we went abroad. Holidays were very important to us, it was nice to get away. We went to London one year, without the children. It was grand, I used to get in the car and drive round London, you got lost on purpose and had to find your way back, it was great. When the children were older, we went dancing a lot, we went to Aysgarth and Masham, all over, to old time dances with live bands. Ours was a different world, we had plenty of work and plenty of interests. Life is different but it is no better now.

I was very fortunate, Coverhead was a good farm. After twenty years of renting, we bought the farm – 3,500 acres plus the farmhouse, buildings and a cottage – for £32,000. But we sold it to some people from down Oxford way in 1983 so we could buy our sons a farm each, one in the village and one half a mile out. We brought them up in the business. If you are born into farming, even in this day, you follow farming. I retired 18 years ago, at 70 years old, due to ill health. But I am there if I am needed, farming is in my heart.

Ronnie Suttill, 61, lives with his wife Margaret at Town End Farm, a four-bedroomed 300-year-old stone farmhouse in Carlton. The couple have two sons, David, 37, who works on the family farm, and Keith, 35, an agricultural engineer. They have 1,200 sheep and 80 cows on 1,100 acres.

Things have changed a lot, I don't think they have changed for the worse, really, they are just different. You have a better standard of life now than when I went to school. We had gas lights and had to saw logs, cart coal and cut peat. Winters have been a lot easier recently, we would get snowed in for weeks, with ten to fifteen feet snow drifts.

I started on the farm full time when I left school at fifteen. I remember my father having horses, although I never worked with them. I learned to drive when I was about ten. It was a sheep farm, 1,200 to 1,300 sheep, at lambing time we were up at 6.0am and working until it was dark.

The big rise in property values is one of the biggest changes I have seen. When I went to school I knew everyone in the dale. There was nobody coming to live from outside like there is now. Where I was born, at Braidley, there were four farms, now there is only one. There are lots of holiday homes, people who come maybe once a month. It is sad but you have to accept it. I only know about half the people in the dale now.

Girls have been moving away from the area for the last twenty years. Farming families tend to stay on, but there are a lot less of them. There are a lot less farms and a lot less people working on them. It all started in the Sixties, in a small way. We all had a chance of buying old houses for nothing. Nobody wanted them then, they were run down, derelict, a bit of a liability. Young couples wanted to live in new houses in places like Leyburn.

When we bought this farm in the village, the house, which had been empty for about eighteen months, was more or less thrown in, it was of no value, just part of the farm. Now the house is worth more than land. It would have been worth less than £10,000 in the early eighties. Houses then were going for £4,000 to £5,000, maybe £14,000 for a big one. We had to build houses on our land for our sons, it was the only way we could afford property in the area. We tried to buy a house in the village for £90,000 in the early nineties but it wanted a lot spending on it. We tried for two barn conversions, but couldn't get planning permission. A house like our eldest son David's would have cost about £150,000 to buy at the time but we were able, using our own stone, to build it on our land for £50,000. It is worth about £300,000 now. The whole farm, with the two houses, is probably worth about £1 million.

Lots of people in the dale have had to build, but it is very difficult to get planning permission. They should have an area in the main village and build half a dozen houses for local people with kiddies. Plenty of people would be willing to let them have land.

It was sad when the village school closed. Me and my wife fought hard to keep it open. We complained, we went to meetings, went to the education people at North Yorkshire County Council on several occasions but it didn't make any difference. When I went there were about three classes, possibly eighty kids. But then it went down to about thirty-five kids, with two teachers. When the school closed something went from the village, there were no nativities, no concerts. Once the kids have moved out into another area they are missing for five days a week. It was a big loss.

There were four shops but we have lost them all now too. There are just the mini-supermarkets in Leyburn. We used to have a butcher van and a grocery van, even a country clothing van come regularly, but they stopped about 20 years ago. Things have come full circle now, the Tesco van comes all this way to do home deliveries for £5. Churches and chapels have closed too. The older generation is dying off and young people don't tend to go. We were made to go to Sunday School every week, we walked three miles there, and three back if our parents didn't come. I enjoyed it, we met other kids.

We got a new village hall in the sixties, there's badminton and bowls there, and events at Christmas, there's still quite a community spirit, if someone's having a fortieth birthday party everyone's invited. I have only been away on about four big holidays but we get away for weekends, now there's two of us working on the farm.

(Opposite) Two photographs of Horsehouse, the highest village in Coverdale, taken half a century apart. Little appears to have changed in the sense that the shop and post office depicted in the lower picture are still there in the background of the present-day photograph – as is the traditional phone box. Missing from the current scene is the vicar talking to his parishioners. Alf Suttill recalls: "There used to be two churches in Horsehouse – there isn't one now. One is a house – the other is being converted into a house." (Mike Kipling Photography [top])

Alf Suttill and his family in the hayfield in the summer of 2000. Left to right are: grandson John; Alf; son Ronnie; grandson David; great granddaughter Harriet; and son Malcolm.

We've seen a lot of changes in farming too. The best thing that ever happened in the Dales was the introduction of the round baler for silage. Years ago, hay-making was a lot of hard work. The introduction of fertilisers from the mid-sixties means we can grow a lot more grass now and we are not so dependent on the weather. We used to be working all of July and early August until 11pm at night hay-making, and you had to leave it for six days to wilt. All that work and it could just be destroyed by the weather. Many other things have been made easier too. We clipped the sheep by hand when we started, then we had a petrol engine clipper and electric in the mid-Fifties. The trailers are bigger and better and lighter too. Taking cattle to market used to be so much harder. We now use two or three big tractors for muckspreading. We used to lead it out in trailers and spread it.

BSE and Foot and Mouth – that was the beginning of the bad years. But I never thought of giving up. When you've got animals, they've got to be looked after and fed. The prices went down so much, I did wonder if it was all worth it, but we were owners, not renters, we couldn't afford to sell out, we would have had nothing. Foot and mouth was only five miles away, you never knew if you were going to get it. We lost a couple of sheep after they strayed into the wrong area. The restrictions were hard, not being able to go anywhere. We had two hundred sheep stuck down in Suffolk, they had been down there grazing for the winter. I was confident we would come out of it, you have got to think positive or you would go out of business. We're in it for the long haul.

I don't know if my grandchildren will continue with farming, it is changing with each generation. If you were born in the dale in the forties and fifties, you didn't have any choice, the majority of people started on the farm after school. There are other options now, they might be better off outside farming, working five days a week, forty hours. It is no good encouraging them to do farming if they are not happy.

David Suttill, 37, lives in a three-bedroom stone house in Carlton, which his family built on their land in 1995. He has a three-year-old daughter, Harriet, who lives with her mother in Newcastle.

Our village school closed when I still had one more year to do, so I had to go to Middleham for my last year. I started work on the farm at Coverhead at sixteen. My school friends, the lads from farming backgrounds, are all still in the area. They were all born to it, it is a way of life. Pride and family ties keep them in the area. But the girls have moved away. Most of them went to college initially and didn't come back. About sixty to seventy per cent have stayed away, there is no work for them. When we were younger, we had to travel twenty-five miles to places like Skipton to go to nightclubs and meet people. A lot of lads have married girls from outside. There are not a lot of locals left.

Village life is non-existent, we hardly know anyone in the village, half the houses are only lived in as holiday cottages or second homes, we don't mix. There were three or four shops in the dale when I was younger, there aren't any now. People in holiday cottages come with their cars full of groceries from Morrisons and Asda. You don't see them in local pubs. There were three or four shops in the dale when I was younger, there aren't any now.

We go to the local pub to play darts on Tuesday nights. I have also done a lot of mountain bike trialling. I first went on a ski trip with school at fourteen and have been on about fifteen skiing holidays with friends to France and Italy since. Laying on a beach doesn't appeal to me. The pace of life seems to have got faster, people have more money to spend.

But most locals couldn't afford to buy houses in the village now. We thought they were expensive twenty years ago, but it turned out not. Prices went even higher. A bungalow on my lane was up for sale in the early eighties for about £12,000. Everybody thought that was far too much. Then it went on the market six years ago for £190,000. But I have always said it's no good looking over the fence, you are no better when you get there. Folk living here do two hours travelling to Leeds or Teesside to work thirty-five hours a week. I take my hat off to anybody who can do that. We work seventy, eighty and ninety hours a week sometimes. But I wouldn't do that sort of travelling.

The end product is, the quality of life is tremendous. Nobody leaves here to live in the city, they all come the other way.

We're having to work harder over the last ten years for the same income. Everybody has more livestock now than they did in the seventies. My granddad used to go out and buy a new Land Rover or tractors when he wanted. Workwise it was easier because it wasn't as intensive as it is now. Then, he had 1,600 sheep on about 4,000 acres. Twenty years ago we had 350 sheep and 25 cows. Now we have 1,200 sheep and 80 cows on 1,000 acres. We work seven days a week now, if we're lucky in winter we get a few hours off on a Sunday, in summer we have no hours off. There was a time when they didn't work on a Sunday at all, they didn't need to. And they had to rest the horses.

It would be nice to be able to employ someone. We sometimes have casual help but we have to do ninety per cent of the work ourselves. We have modernised in many ways, putting new buildings up to hold more and more livestock. My granddad walked across the fields to tend to the sheep, I remember trying to keep up with him as a kid, he used to go like the clappers. I use a quad bike now. We're using a lot more fertiliser and we have mowing machines that buzz the grass off like a lawn mower. Machinery like the round baler makes it easier to make silage. We're not reliant on hay any more.

Income is a bit better this year, but Foot and Mouth was a disaster, it was the worst time, not going anywhere, waiting for something to happen. It was costing a lot of money to keep sheep alive and we were selling livestock off at a big loss, giving them away basically. It's better now, but nobody's getting fat off it. We kept going, we had to look after the animals. I think it is a lot to do with the area you are in, it is a very proud area, you can see it is a proud area by the quality of the stock that goes through the auction marts. It is a part of you, you might feel like giving up but it is in you.

I don't know if the next generation will want to go into farming. There are a lot more opportunities for them, there weren't so many for us twenty years ago. We felt farming was the only option. Although I want them to have opportunities, I would like to see somebody from the family go into farming. I would back them one hundred per cent.

Travelling around the Dales Then and Now

Colin Speakman

The 1950s - end of an era

Imagine a little country railway station in the Yorkshire Dales in the early 1950s. A near deserted platform, perhaps just a couple of people waiting for the single late afternoon train. There might be a few empty milk churns on the platform, together with a couple of trunks on a long porter's barrow, with PLA (Passengers Luggage in Advance) labels pasted on them, perhaps belonging to a holidaymaker returning home and a student going away to college. The station would be staffed, with a single railwayman combining duties of booking clerk and porter. The buildings would have a run down, neglected look, even though it was part of the recently nationalised British Railway with some new posters and notices on old LMS or LNER notice boards.

The train when it arrived would be hauled by an elderly tank or mixed traffic tender engine, wheezing steam, hauling a couple of non-corridor coaches, complete with faded view of Whitby harbour over long, musty bench-type passenger seats, and a huge leather strap to open the window.

A couple of people would alight, the two trunks hauled into the guard's van with a few friendly quips between the guard and driver, and with little more than a nod from the porter, the train would, with a hiss of steam, ease slowly away. The passengers would depart, the porter return to his office for a little form filling and a cigarette, and peace would descend as the chuffing of the engine disappeared, round the bend, out of earshot, drowned by birdsong.

A timeless scene, which in essence had changed little from late Victorian England. You can almost recreate such a scene on the Embsay Steam Railway, with one important difference - there'll be lots more passengers around than ever were using rural railways at the end of the steam era.

Closures and cutbacks

It was all about to change. On 24th April, 1954, just six months before the establishment of the Yorkshire Dales as a National Park, the last passenger train left Garsdale station for Northallerton along the Wensleydale line - though for a few days during the terrible winter of 1963 when roads were blocked by snowdrifts trains ran an emergency service to take milk and passengers.

"The train would be hauled by an elderly tank engine, wheezing steam, hauling a couple of non-corridor coaches. A couple of people would alight, the train would ease slowly away and peace would descend". End of an era at Hawes as a Garsdale to Northallerton train calls just prior to the withdrawal of through services in 1954.

How it might have been! Great rejoicing in September 1958 when the Leeds Publicity Club ran a special diesel train to Hawes, outward via Ripon and Northallerton and back via Settle. Cafés and inns in Hawes were besieged during the four-hour stay and the 200 passengers bought large quantities of Wensleydale cheese. The station buildings on the right now form part of the Dales Countryside Museum.

Packed excursion trains were for many years a feature of the Grassington branch at Bank Holidays. A return working to Bradford is preparing to leave the terminus on Easter Monday 1950.

Arten Gill viaduct, painted by Chris Wade (opposite), is symbolic of the dramatic splendour of the Settle – Carlisle railway. The same viaduct (above) is being crossed in June 1966 by a diesel unit on one of the stopping services that were withdrawn in 1970. (Colour-Rail/Bill Chapman)

Hawes station was to remain open for another five years with just a single daily train between Bradford and Hawes. A few weeks before the closure of the Wensleydale line, in January 1954, the route through the Lune valley between Clapham and Tebay had also closed. Stations at Ingleton Kirkby Lonsdale, Barbon, Sedbergh, and Low Gill saw their last trains, though Ingleton was used by occasional excursion trains. The Grassington branch to Threshfield had long closed to passengers (in 1930), but remained open for freight, including stone from the two quarries served by the branch, though Grassington station was also brought back to life once or twice a year with packed ramblers' excursion trains.

The other major change on the rail network within the Dales was the replacement of steam by more cost-efficient diesel trains, most especially by diesel railcars on the surviving lines. These included local trains along the scenic Settle-Carlisle line, the "Little" North Western between Leeds, Skipton and Morecambe, and the direct line between Ilkley and Skipton via Bolton Abbey and

Embsay. Other cost savings included taking staff away from all local stations, but this also meant loss of the local parcel and luggage facility as well as the security of a friendly face to sell you a ticket or deal with enquiries in the booking office.

But worse was to come. Dr Richard Beeching's notorious report on the Reshaping of British Railways, published in 1963, proposed the closure of every railway and every station within the Dales. Within a couple of years, Bolton Abbey and Embsay stations on the Ilkley-Skipton line were closed (now happily restored as part of the Embsay Steam Railway). Local stations between Settle and Appleby were also due to close in 1964, but were reprieved only to be finally closed in 1970. The entire line with its freight and through express passenger trains only survived because of its value as a relief line whilst the West Coast main line was being electrified during the early 1970s. Ironically, local stations on the Leeds-Morecambe line such as Gargrave, Hellifield, Long Preston, Giggleswick and Clapham only survived

Swaledale long kept its own bus operator – Percivals. One of their fleet waits at Reeth around midday in the early 1950s. There is virtually no other sign of life, which was nothing unusual in this era.

because the decision was taken to close the far busier Skipton-Colne link in 1970, and these lightly used stations survived by default.

Apart from a small handful of rail enthusiasts and environmentalists, few people protested about the loss of these rural railways. There was a general assumption that railways, especially railways in country areas, were an outmoded form of transport, overtaken by progress, and the future lay with more cost-effective buses but most all with the freedom and flexibility offered by the private car.

The Rise - and Fall - of the Bus network

The petrol and later diesel bus offered many advantages over the country railway. It wasn't confined to a track but could use any part of what, by the 1950s, was a greatly improved, tarmac road network. It was cheaper to operate than even a diesel railcar and had greater flexibility. If it was a good deal slower than a train, it could also serve town and village centres, not some isolated station up to four miles away from the village it was supposed to serve. This made it more popular with most users - at least until they had access to their own car.

In fact during the immediate post war years, a time of austerity, rationing and shortages, car ownership was a luxury enjoyed by only a better-off minority of the population. In comparison it was a golden era for the bus, which for a decade or so was the dominant form of transport within the Dales for local people and visitors alike.

From humble beginnings as horse-drawn waggonette operators, local firms such as Chapman's of Grassington, who initially ran a daily horse bus and mail coach service between Skipton railway station, Grassington and Buckden, were soon operating modern charabancs and motor bus services. During the inter-war years a comprehensive network of bus services evolved in the Dales. Initially this was to complement the rail services, collecting passengers at stations to serve the hinterland where railways never ran. But this was soon to compete against and eventually replace the railway.

By the 1950s, a series of amalgamations and by-outs had produced three or four major companies who were to dominate transport provision in the Dales for more than thirty years. In the south-east, operating out of the West Yorkshire conurbation and Harrogate, was the West Yorkshire Road Car Company, with a large fleet of vehicles. To the north-east, out of Darlington and Northallerton, was the United group, though Swaledale kept its own local operator, Percivals, for many years. To the west and north-west into Lancashire and what is now Cumbria, Ribble Motors dominated, though in Malhamdale and Ribblesdale a smaller local undertaking, Pennine Motors, which still survives as an independent operator, served Malham, Settle and jointly with Ribble, villages along the main A65.

Services on weekdays, at least, if slow by twenty-first century standards, were reasonably frequent. Wensleydale, for example, had regular services between Leyburn and Hawes, along both the south and northern side of the dale, via Redmire and Askrigg, or West Burton

Pennine Motors still survives as an independent operator. A bus built in 1936 and acquired second-hand in 1951 is about to depart from Skipton for Settle. (Donald Binns)

and Aysgarth, and for years buses would interchange at Leyburn.

But soon the bus network too was under increasing pressure from the private car, or as most people perceived it, their own personal as opposed to shared public transport.

The car is triumphant

It now seems self-evident that the car can offer an individual and their family or friends, freedom from the dictates of a timetable that no train or bus can ever match. You can go where you want when you want. You can carry luggage with you, not only suitcases and heavy shopping, but everything you need for a day out - picnic tables and chairs, pets and pushchairs. If you have a disability and can't walk far the car gets you there quickly and easily. No need to stand at windy, rainy bus stops or station platforms hoping the bus or train will turn up on time. Once you have bought and insured your car, the marginal cost of petrol is a fraction of what a trip to the Dales will cost in bus or rail fares. Such costs have declined in favour of the motorist over the last fifty years, as cars have become relatively cheaper to own, maintain and operate compared with the relatively high costs of rural bus fares.

As Britain's economy recovered from the austerity of the post-war years, and incomes rose, the first luxury item that most families wanted to buy was their own personal freedom - a car.

Compared with the relatively expensive and unreliable vehicles of the pre-war years, the new generation of initially British-built cars - the Morris Minor, the Austin Popular, the ubiquitous Mini, the Ford Anglia, the Triumph Herald, all soon to be overtaken by foreign competition - offered new standards of speed and comfort for personal travel. From around four million cars and vans on Britain's roads in 1950, by 1960 this had more than doubled to around nine million, but by 1970 this had almost grown to twelve million. The growth in the last three decades has been even more spectacular and now stands at around twenty-three million, with much of the growth being in two and three car households.

The implication for the Yorkshire Dales of this rapid growth in car ownership and usage has been enormous. For most families in Britain, the car has been an enormous liberator, offering a wide choice of where to live and work, and having a huge impact on leisure patterns. People can now live in isolated hamlets in the upper Dales, and still commute daily to Leeds, Bradford, Darlington, Lancaster, Preston or even Manchester by an ever improving road network.

Over the last fifty years, car ownership within the Yorkshire Dales has expanded from being the privilege of the affluent few to becoming something most of the

The creation of a greatly improved tarmac road network paved the way for the bus and the private car. Much road work was then carried out by steam rollers that undoubtedly possessed great character. In an unusual choice of subject, the Wensleydale artist Robert Nicholls has depicted one such roller at the top of Howgate, near Askrigg.

population enjoy. Although it is not quite true to say that "everyone has a car in the Dales" (around 15% of households do not own a car), never has the majority of the population in the Dales enjoyed such a high degree of personal mobility, with nearly half of households having two or more cars. Outside the Dales, something like three-quarters of the population of the major catchment towns and cities, which means that over ninety per cent of visitors to the Dales come by car. On any fine weekend this fact is self evident.

As well as having huge significance for all leisure activity in the Dales, this high degree of mobility has other effects, not all equally welcome.

On the positive side, people living in the Dales are no longer physically isolated in the way they were two generations ago. Most local people, providing they can drive, now enjoy virtually identical access to shops, cultural facilities and services as their urban counterparts. True, travel times may be significantly

longer, and at certain times of the year journeys may be problematic because of poor weather. But generally speaking, thanks to wide car ownership and high quality roads, it is now possible to enjoy the benefits of living in a beautiful area such as the Yorkshire Dales National Park and enjoying easy access to most sports, cultural and retail facilities in nearby towns and cities.

This itself has a negative side, because if you can do your shopping in an urban hypermarket half an hour's drive away where prices are perhaps twenty-five per cent cheaper than the village shop, and the range of goods almost infinite, local shops find it increasingly difficult to compete. To some degree, local traders are compensated by visitors who, in the summer months at least, may patronise local shops and services and help make up the loss of local resident patronage. The same is true of rural garages which cannot compete with cut-price supermarket forecourts where most locals will fill their tanks; several village garages have closed in the Upper Dales over the last few years.

Malham during Easter week 1959 with just a handful of cars on the village green. The main tourist season did not then begin until Whitsuntide (now the Spring Bank Holiday). Also still in the future was the real car invasion of the Dales, which brought with it the construction of a large car park and visitor centre. Associated road widening enabled drivers to approach weekend congestion at speed. (David Joy)

This high degree of personal mobility, allowing those people living in the Dales to enjoy the best of both worlds, has produced ever-increasing competition for housing. People, usually older people with higher incomes or capital to invest and a good retirement pension, move into the area and outbid local people, especially younger people, even if they are employed in the village, for available housing. The result is a constant housing boom in the Dales, with inevitable pressure to release ever more land for building or to allow more conversion of barns for luxury housing, even in isolated locations. An older, more affluent population means a declining birth rate with less need for schools, and many of these have closed or faced closure with declining rolls.

On the other hand, the incomers are often among the most enthusiastic supporters of local societies and community activity. Paradoxically, many younger workers with jobs within the National Park, for example in catering or building, now have to drive in each day from peripheral towns where housing costs are cheaper, which easy access to their own transport also makes possible.

Public transport fights back

The switch to the private car over the last half-century has meant ever reducing regular patronage for the surviving rail services and buses, with a familiar spiral of decline through the 1960s and 1970s. In order to make up decreasing fare revenue, bus companies increased fares and cut their services to meet costs. Faced with a worsening and more expensive service, many Dales families even of limited means were persuaded to acquire their own car, even if it had to be a second-hand vehicle. This meant even less regular travellers, thus perpetuating yet more cuts.

Sunday services were usually the first to go, making whole areas of the Dales inaccessible for local people and visitors alike on the days when most people had time

(Above)   *Financial support has enabled the Dalesbus network to continue and even expand. Evening shadows are falling as an Arriva service waits at Malham.*

(Left)   *Also operated by Arriva is the highly innovative Dales Bike Bus, which brings cyclists and their mounts from Wakefield via Leeds, Otley and Ilkley. It is seen at Grassington, with the National Park Centre on the left and state-of-the-art bus shelter on the right.* (Colin Speakman - 2)

available for leisure activity, again another incentive to acquire a car. By the 1980s, most bus services in the Dales were reduced to a skeletal network, running during the daytime on weekdays only. These services only existed because of school buses, which between the morning and afternoon school runs were available to provide some shopping trips for that small minority too poor or old to run a car.

Thankfully, Sunday bus services did not quite disappear in the southern Dales, mainly thanks to the West Yorkshire Road Car Company. With a fleet of vehicles available for weekend services that were used on weekdays in the nearby conurbations of West Yorkshire, it saw a marketing opportunity in the summer months. This was not only to continue their historic market day buses over the Kidstone Pass between Skipton and Hawes and Leyburn, linking Wharfedale and Wensleydale, but to operate what was soon to be known as the Dalesbus network. This was mainly based on a direct leisure bus service from Leeds and Bradford to Ilkley and Bolton Abbey, then to Grassington and over the Kidstone Pass to Aysgarth and Hawes, and either over the Buttertubs Pass to Keld in Swaledale or via Ribblehead to Ingleton.

Though the economics of bus operation, including

drivers' hours regulations, have made it impossible in recent years to operate the Dalesbus service purely commercially, financial support from the National Park Authority, the Countryside Agency and North Yorkshire County Council has allowed the Dalesbus network to continue and even expand. There have also been spectacular improvements in provision of the weekday network in the Dales in recent years, mainly due to the Government's Rural Bus Grant to North Yorkshire County Council. This has allowed many traditional bus services in the Dales to be restored and expanded to historically high levels, in most cases with modern, low floor vehicles which improve passenger comfort, especially for older people, parents with children and buggies, and those with disabilities. There are also Rural Transport Partnerships based in both Craven and in Richmondshire, which have helped fill in the gaps that conventional buses cannot meet, for example with community dial-a-bus services, shared taxis and car hire. There has yet to be any attempt to use these same services to meet the needs of visitors as well as local people, thus boosting both revenue and local economic benefit.

All this has done much to reverse the trends, with a significant increase in the number of local people and visitors using the new bus network. Whilst patronage will never reach pre-motoring age levels, there is now a reasonable enough public transport network available to allow people to reach and travel most of the area without the need for a car. Yet important gaps in the network remain if it is truly to compete with the convenience of the car, for example for evening journeys and during winter weekends.

Support for both local and leisure public transport has grown in recent years. This reflects a growing recognition that, whilst the private car will provide the backbone of travel for the majority of people both to and within the Dales for the foreseeable future, there will always be a significant minority of people who for whatever reason - income, health, youth, age or simply inclination - do not have access to a car or do not drive. This also includes many overseas visitors who don't choose to bring or hire a car yet want to discover the Yorkshire Dales. Such people are important contributors to the local economy.

At the same time it is also recognised that the car itself brings major environmental and social problems, not just those of congestion, which is mainly limited to a few busy Sunday afternoons in honey pot locations in the Dales. More serious and long term are various forms of pollution, including air pollution, a major contribution of

human illness, ecological damage and global warming, visual pollution in protected landscapes or conservation areas caused by the impact of lines of parked cars and noise pollution in otherwise tranquil areas. Perhaps most insidious of all, the danger of speeding traffic on narrow roads has caused walking or cycling to be perceived as dangerous.

While many of these problems need tackling at source through cleaner and quieter engines (especially motor cycles), or by traffic management measures to control speeds and parking on minor roads and in sensitive locations, it is also important to create a viable alternative. Visitors will then believe that they have a real choice as well as the opportunity to drive to the Dales or to leave their cars at home or at a safe, off-road location such as a railway station car park and to take the bus or train. Public transport can also offer the opportunity for ramblers prepared to plan ahead to undertake linear walks, for example dale to dale, along a ridge or to undertake a section of a long distance paths such as the Dales Way or Pennine Way, without the nuisance and pollution of two cars and two drivers.

The alternative to the car - the Dales Rail story

Proof that this can be achieved was demonstrated in the 1970s when the Yorkshire Dales National Park Committee, as it was then, took the bold step of helping to finance the repair of what at that time were five disused station platforms at key railway stations on the magnificent Settle-Carlisle line in or close to the National Park - Horton, Ribblehead, Dent, Garsdale and Kirkby Stephen. In May 1975 the first of a series of monthly weekend charter trains, known as Dales Rail, was operated on Saturdays and Sundays between Leeds and Bradford and Appleby. Fares were deliberately kept low to match the marginal costs of driving a car and, amazing as it seems now, two people could spend a day in the Dales by Dales Rail for about the same cost as a couple of gallons of petrol. In 1976 the service was extended to Carlisle, with stations in the Eden Valley (Langwathby, Lazonby and Armathwaite), thanks to support from Cumbria County Council. In 1977 the service was extended from Lancashire with Clitheroe station being reopened, initially on an experimental basis.

A fundamental part of the Dales Rail concept was an integrated rail and bus service, which met trains at Garsdale station and served Sedbergh and Hawes, with extensions to Barbondale or the Howgills and into Swaledale. Equally important was a programme of

(Opposite, top) *The inaugural Dales Rail service calls at Garsdale in May 1975. Waiting on the platform are many dalesfolk about to enjoy their first trip by train since the withdrawal of stopping services five years earlier.* (David Joy)

(Lower) *The development of passenger services over the Settle-Carlisle line has enabled walkers to plan linear routes, outward by train and back on foot or vice versa. Participants in a Yorkshire Dales Society walk are overlooking the line near Ais Gill as they take a rest.*

(This page) *A Carlisle service pauses at Dent - highest station on the Settle-Carlisle line - in the summer of 1994.* (Colin Speakman - 2)

guided walks with every train and bus service, so that rather than being dropped in the middle of a perhaps unfamiliar environment, experienced volunteer guides would take walkers into the heart of the National Park. Dales Rail users were a captive market and could be encouraged on their day out to share an awareness of National Park purposes and the need to travel in more sustainable ways.

The success of Dales Rail in the late '70s was phenomenal, with trains being fully booked on numerous occasions, and services being expanded in frequency each year. There was even a special Christmas shoppers' service in December to help Dales people reach the busy shops of Leeds or Carlisle, which was also used by hardy winter walkers.

There is little doubt that Dales Rail, though only a weekend service - by the 1980s it was fortnightly in the main season - saved the Settle-Carlisle line. It built up a huge new market of people who were regularly using trains along the threatened main Midland line to visit the Dales, mainly for walking. Compared with the handful of dedicated enthusiasts using the regular scheduled service, several thousand passengers on the Dales Rail trains were quick to join the protest movement of the early 1980s. This arose when British Railways announced the imminent closure of the line, primarily because of the alleged massive costs of restoring the landmark Ribblehead viaduct.

The battle to save the Settle-Carlisle has been well documented elsewhere. In the mid- 1980s it became a major national issue. Crucial was the legal decision that Dales Rail stations, as they currently enjoyed publicly advertised rail services, were legally "open". This allowed many thousands of committed Dales Rail users to protest, as they did in very large numbers with an unprecedented 22,000 registered objectors, plus one dog, against the withdrawal of a facility they valued so highly. It became a major political battle. The value of the line and its users had to the local rural economy was finally recognised. On 11th April 1989, the Minister of Transport at that time, Michael Portillo, gave the decision that everyone was waiting for, and England's most spectacular main line was reprieved.

Cumbria County Council had already broken new ground in 1986 by financing what was initially a daily charter service along the line, using the Dales Rail precedent, aiming to get young people to school and college in Carlisle from local stations in the Eden valley. Instead of a few weekend Dales Rail trains, there was now a daily service, every two to three hours, along the entire line. Both the Friends of the Settle-Carlisle - who had led the campaign to save the line - and the Friends of Dales Rail co-operated to provide guided walks off the weekend trains. Publicity surrounding the closure had boosted travel on the line to around 500,000 passengers a year, making the "S&C" one of the region's top tourist attractions, bringing visitors and their spending power from all over the UK and overseas. However the walkers, often filling the trains on winter weekends when few

others are travelling, and spending their time and money in the National Park rather than just travelling through, remained vital customers.

Lancashire County Council has continued to promote the Sunday rail services from Blackpool and Manchester, using the Blackburn-Hellifield line which is now open to regular weekday passenger trains as far as Clitheroe. They have kept the Dales Rail brand name and, with the name, a fully integrated bus network into Wensleydale and Swaledale, together with a comprehensive programme of guided walks.

There was even an attempt, in 1977, by the National Park Committee to launch a similar integrated rail and bus service on the surviving section of the Wensleydale Railway between Redmire and Northallerton, which after initial success, failed because of a lack of political will. However, in 2003, the Wensleydale Railway Company who had just purchased the line from Network Rail, successfully launched a service between Leyburn and Bedale, which it is hoped, over the coming decade, will be extended to Northalleton, Redmire, Aysgarth and eventually to Hawes and Garsdale. It would thus restore a vital, scenic trans-Pennine link which would provide a real alternative to the car to reach and travel through the Dales.

Protecting the Dales rural road and lane network - a landscape feature

Despite the importance of the rail network, travel in the Yorkshire Dales has always been primarily dependent on its complex network of paths, tracks and minor roads which criss-cross the whole of the National Park like a complex spider's web. These routes have evolved, mainly for pedestrian and horse traffic, from the earliest days of settlement in the area to the present day - and are still evolving.

The modern road network, with the notable exception of a handful of turnpike roads through Ribblesdale, Wharfedale and Wensleydale, derives largely from this ancient pattern of trackways and winding lanes. During the late eighteenth and early nineteenth century period of enclosures, when the complex pattern of drystone walls and scattered barns emerged as such a distinctive and internationally recognised feature of the Yorkshire Dales landscape, these walled lanes, some of them extremely narrow, became a key feature of that landscape.

But with the road traffic growth in the 1960s and '70s, there was real concern by the 1970s that many of these lanes and country roads would disappear or be changed beyond recognition by road improvement and widening schemes. Successive county council highway engineers were carrying out piecemeal improvement schemes, usually on alleged safety grounds, straightening roads by removing a bend here or there, widening verges, putting down urban style concrete kerbs and removing historic walls. This has happened not just along the main A65 trunk road to the south of the National Park, but along the two main quarry access roads, the B6479 and B6265, along Ribblesdale and Wharfedale. The main A684 through Wensleydale has suffered several urbanising widening schemes, which simply serve to encourage speeding traffic and more accidents elsewhere. There was even serious talk about a Hawes by-pass and signing a link through the National Park from the M6 to the A1 via the A684. This would have resulted in a non-stop procession of heavy lorries going through the heart of the National Park, and consequent demands for yet more huge and unsightly road improvement schemes.

It was these concerns which led the local branch of the Council for the Protection of Rural England to produce, in 1974, a pamphlet about the need to conserve the special character of Dales roads as a key feature of the unique landscape heritage of the area. This was influential in the production of an Advisory Hierarchy of Roads in the Yorkshire Dales National Park. The Yorkshire Dales National Park Committee and North Yorkshire County Council formally adopted this important document in 1981, in full consultation with Cumbria County Council. It recognised that motor traffic, whether commercial or private, had to fit into the unique environment of the National Park rather than the other way about. It was realised that there was neither need nor justification for through commercial traffic through the Dales, as the National Park enjoyed the benefit of being within what can be described as a Trunk Road/Motorway box, formed

(Opposite) *Serious concern in the 1960s about landscape damage caused by so-called road improvement schemes led to the Council for the Protection of Rural England devising a "road hierarchy". It identified many minor roads where no further widening or "improvement" should take place. Justifiably among them was the magnificent route across the tops from Arncliffe to Malham, here painted by Chris Wade as it begins the descent to Darnbrook.*

by the M6 to the west, the A66/A685 to the north, the A61/A1(M) to the east and the A65/A59 to the south, all outside the borders of the National Park.

It was fully accepted that local residents need a safe, well-maintained network to access this motorway/trunk road box, but this does not need to be high speed. Nor is the Hierarchy based on formal highway classification, but on the actual function of the roads in terms of giving people access to and from the area as well as travelling within the Dales. The categories are therefore based on the actual work the roads do, and also their landscape character. This classification divided Dales roads, lanes and tracks into Primary, Secondary and Tertiary distributors, local and access roads and green lanes. In principle the lower the category of road, the greater degree of protection it should receive in terms of its special character and environmental quality. The lower categories are perceived as being largely for local residents' needs or less intrusive forms of recreation such as walking and cycling.

Over the last two decades the Advisory Hierarchy has served the National Park well, ensuring that no major unsightly road improvement schemes, apart from minor safety schemes, have taken place. The winding Dales roads have been protected as an integral and characteristic part of the landscape. It has also proved how highway engineers and National Park officers can work closely together to achieve common aims.

The challenge ahead

While road traffic has increased in the Dales over the last half century, it has not increased as quickly over the last two decades as many people feared. If anything visitor travel patterns may have levelled off as a result of many factors - cheap holidays overseas, changing leisure patterns including the growth of Sunday shopping and new retail outlets and Sunday spectator sports. If this means less traffic pressure on narrow Dales roads, this is to be welcomed. However it still does not remove the need, first and foremost, to ensure that good traffic management measures are in place throughout the National Park, and secondly to ensure that there is a truly viable network of affordable, attractive and more sustainable alternatives. These must include making best possible use of the rail network - the Settle-Carlisle and Morecambe lines, the Wensleydale line and eventually the extension of the Embsay Railway up to Grassington.

Sustainable tourism is essentially about allowing people to move around to experience and enjoy the Dales in the most sustainable way possible, which is on foot, on horseback and by cycle, and wherever possible using and supporting existing local public transport networks rather than adding to pollution and congestion by private car.

So there is a need to make even better use of the Dales bus network, to have a network which is truly competitive with the private car in terms of both quality of experience and cost. It must be fully integrated with the rail network, which will continue to provide the most effective, congestion-free means of travel to and from the nearby major centres of population. Such a network must also be of equal value to the local community as to visitors. It must also integrate fully with the National Park walking and cycling network, again to be available for locals and visitors alike, so that living within the Dales as well as visiting the area without a car becomes, once again, a realistic option.

Despite many fine achievements over the last few years, we are still a long way short of achieving a truly sustainable transport network for the Dales and this is perhaps one of the most difficult and demanding challenges in the years ahead.

Enjoying the Yorkshire Dales
Colin Speakman

A Leisure Landscape

It is fashionable to describe the Yorkshire Dales as a working countryside, recognising the importance of agriculture, forestry, mining and quarrying as activities which have shaped the landscape we see today. Yet it is equally true that, at least since Norman times, much of the Dales has been a leisure landscape. The great hunting Forests or Chases of the higher Dales were for centuries the preserves of an elite who enjoyed the hunting of wild boar and red deer. Vast areas of open moorland and parkland have been shaped, fashioned and conserved by what was essentially a recreational use of that countryside. In more recent times, grouse shooting has enabled huge areas of the gritstone moors to the east and south of the National Park to be carefully managed, as dramatically beautiful heather moors, to enable the maintenance of high populations of black and red grouse for annual shoots.

Field sports remain important in the Yorkshire Dales, from grouse and pheasant shooting in and around the great estates to angling for trout and even salmon along the rivers of the National Park.

What National Parks were set up to achieve, and what the Yorkshire Dales has achieved over the last fifty years has been a democratisation of the use of this great leisure landscape. This has meant allowing everyone, not just the most privileged sections of society, to enjoy the natural beauty and man-made heritage of one of Britain's great cultural landscapes.

Waymarking in progress on Barden Moor, once the sole preserve of shooting parties but now a designated area of Open Countryside. Carrying out the work in 1965 is Wilf Proctor, Warden for the West Riding section of the National Park and then its only full-time employee. He was one of over 500 applicants for the job. (David Joy)

The 1949 Act and Access in the Dales

The 1949 National Parks and Access to the Countryside Act contained several important measures to achieve this. One of the measures of special relevance to the Dales was to set up designated areas of Open Countryside where walkers, subject to sensible restrictions at times of fire risk or during shooting days, could wander freely and enjoy fresh air and exercise. One such area is the heather moorland of the Chatsworth Estate covering Barden Moor and Fell, once the preserve of royal and aristocratic shooting parties. It is perhaps fitting that during the lifetime of the Yorkshire Dales National Park it should have become one of the best examples in the North of England of well managed

(Above) *The heather-covered Barden Moor at its finest. Here walkers now share a sense of open space and wilderness with water gathering grounds, sheep grazing, nature conservation and sporting rights.* (Colin Raw)
(Opposite) *Young aristocrats on the "glorious twelfth". Lord David Belgonie, aged 13 (left), and his friend at Eton, the Hon Harry Orde-Powlett (now Lord Bolton), shooting on Apedale Moors, above Wensleydale.*

open public access. Here walkers share a sense of open space and wilderness with important water gathering grounds, sheep grazing, nature conservation interest and sporting rights. Instead of the conflict and protest of the pre-War years, the Chatsworth Estate at Barden has proved how careful planning and compromise can achieve solutions that benefit all parties. It is a model for what might be achieved under the new Countryside and Rights of Way Act 2000, measures that come into play just at the end of the National Park's Golden Jubilee year.

Public Rights of Way

Perhaps the most significant aspect of the great 1949 Act was the requirement, for sometimes reluctant local authorities, to make a permanent or "Definitive" record of all public rights of way – footpaths, bridleways and roads used as public paths. The process of preparing Draft, Provisional and finally Definitive Maps – after a series of Public Inquiries –- took almost twenty years in the Dales between the mid 1950s and the early 1970s, but what finally emerged has had huge implications for recreation. The rich legacy of public paths and byways is both an integral part of the cultural heritage of the Dales and a superb way, in its own right, to experience that heritage, including the rich nature conservation and geological resource which makes the Dales special.

Many of what are now recorded as public paths or bridleways through the Dales date back to prehistoric times, or the earliest days of Anglian and Viking settlement, as vital routes of communication across and

between individual Dales. There are numerous ancient packhorse ways and trade routes which can still be followed on the map on or on foot. Others are more local links, between farms and hamlets, parishioner's ways to and from the village church, peddlers or even postmen's paths, between farms, along the valley side. Some were even created at the time of the Enclosure Acts specifically for recreation to allow people to admire a view or to take the air.

The value of the footpath, bridleway and byway network recorded in the 1950s has increased immeasurably for walkers and cyclists as motor traffic has claimed the tarmac roads. Many walking guides published even as late as the 1930s recommended use of public roads to walk along, as traffic was so light, and in many cases these roads were still unsurfaced tracks. But as traffic increased in both volume and speed, the roads became less and less attractive or safe for non-motorised users, and traffic free paths and off-road trails have become much more appealing.

People were hardly aware of the availability of this rich heritage of walking, riding and cycling routes until the first "One Inch" Ordnance Survey Maps began, in the 1970s, to carry those little red dotted lines indicating where a public right of way ran. Until that time you could never be quite sure if a dotted black line on a map was a right of way and whether or not you had a legal right to be there.

Many of these paths, though recorded by Parish and County Councils, had not in fact been used for years. If anything by the 1950s and '60s their use was still diminishing as local people, acquiring cars, no longer used their local paths to get around or between villages. Many were overgrown and blocked with wire, junk or walls. Farmers and landowners had in many cases forgotten that they existed and often challenged walkers armed with the new OS maps.

Discovering the Dales

But there was a new confidence. The first of a new generation of walking guides began to appear, offering what at that time were little known walking routes through the Dales. Some of them have since become extremely well known and well trodden routes as successive generations of guidebook writers have popularised the Yorkshire Dales as one of Britain's top walking areas.

The transport revolution was also making a difference. Until the 1960s, most ramblers either did their walking close to where they lived, or came out on in the summer months on one of the popular ramblers' excursion trains which operated from Leeds, Bradford and other towns in the old West Riding, and also from Manchester and East Lancashire. A prime purpose of the Area Committees of the Ramblers Association in the 1950s was to negotiate the annual programme of excursion trains with British Railways as it was then known. The RA provided experienced leaders, each with a coloured armband, to take walkers on a series of public hikes varying from around six "easy" to perhaps twelve or thirteen "strenuous" miles in the upper Dales. Regular excursion trains used the Settle – Carlisle, Leeds – Morecambe, Wensleydale and Ingleton – Lowgill lines and even the Grassington branch. There were stories, in the immediate post-war years, of up to a thousand people arriving by train in Grassington and the village being "eaten out" by teatime and the walkers making their way to packed trains back to Leeds or Manchester. In Wharfedale busy summer Sunday trains shuttled from Leeds, Bradford and Ilkley to Bolton Abbey station, again bringing several hundred people into the Dales every Sunday for walking and sightseeing.

But walkers were confined to areas accessible from the station or nearby bus routes, and generally went along well known paths, usually in organised parties, or made use of the network of Youth Hostels, again many of them on popular routes such as the newly established Pennine Way.

The car and access to the footpath network

Rising car ownerships and publication of even more detailed 1:25,000 "Pathfinder" and "Outdoor Leisure" maps meant that for the first time walkers, armed with accurate maps showing where the paths actually were, could get further and deeper into the countryside. You could now walk from your car wherever you could park it. The popularity of the new guidebooks meant that many paths, little used for generations, suddenly became very much busier.

(Opposite) City dweller meets countryman in the 1950s. Brian Clarke (right), on a three-week walking holiday from London, seeks advice from Roland Woodward of Fremington on how to get to Marrick. Huge improvements to the footpath network in recent years have largely removed doubts on where to walk.

(Left) *Malham Cove in Easter week 1959 with scarcely a soul in sight and no obvious sign of a path to the foot of this majestic limestone cliff.*
(David Joy)

(Opposite) *The present-day approach to the Cove. Some may regret the presence of what has been described as a pedestrian motorway, but it is a practical response to the sheer weight of visitor numbers and prevents erosion over a wide area.*
(Granville Harris)

Initially there was conflict as walkers found paths blocked and farmers resented the sudden intrusion of urbanites armed with a maps and demanding to walk paths which until recently had been long overgrown and forgotten. Fortunately there was now a National Park in being to help resolve the problems.

A major achievement of the National Park Authority over the last three decades has been to survey, clear, improve, signpost, waymark and maintain these routes. In some cases this has required legal action to remove anomalies and absurdities by diversion, creation and closure. Huge efforts, by both the Park's own field staff and by Dales Volunteers, have resulted in a well signed and generally waymarked network. Paths are now easy to find, with few if any major problems for the walkers, in stark contrast to many areas outside the National Park where going for a short walk along the footpath network can still be something of an assault course.

Dealing with visitor pressures

The dramatic growth in car ownership in Britain since the 1950s and the impact this would have on leisure patterns is something that the original founding fathers of the National Parks could not have anticipated. Ease of access has dramatically increased the popularity of all forms of car-based tourism, including caravanning and staying at self-catering cottages in what would have been remote areas, well away from a bus route. While this meant that many more people can now enjoy what is perhaps the single most popular leisure activity, a drive through the

Dales, perhaps with a pub lunch or afternoon tea in one of the more attractive villages, increasingly people enjoy much more active forms of recreation. This includes leaving the car and going for a walk or even a cycle ride.

This has meant an increased demand by visitors not only for somewhere to park with toilets, and somewhere for a cup of tea, but somewhere to have an easy circular walk of perhaps three or four miles from the parked vehicle.

The National Park Committee's response to the challenge since the 1960s has been to create just such facilities – a network of car parks and toilets blocks in or near popular villages such as Aysgarth, Clapham, Kettlewell, Buckden, Hawes, Malham, Grassington, Stainforth, Dent and Sedbergh. Because it was felt important to influence visitor behaviour to reduce anticipated problems of litter and vandalism, a network of Visitor Centres were opened at key car parks. These were places where visitors could enjoy a brief introduction to the special qualities of the landscape they were visiting, hopefully also encouraging greater awareness of the fragility of that landscape and the importance of farming. This would encourage more thoughtful and responsible behaviour. The Centre at Aysgarth Falls even had its own café with home made cakes, whilst the small interpretive centre in the old station at Hawes was, in the 1980s expanded into the excellent Dales Countryside Museum with its study and inter-active facilities.

To meet the demand for easy, car-based local walks, a programme of guided "Walks with a Warden" was

arranged from the Centres and a series of self-guided walks leaflets published. The success of these walks can be seen where once indistinct paths in popular areas are now broad and well used. Again, as experience in areas such as Malham and Bolton Abbey/Strid woods has proved, careful path and stile maintenance can prevent erosion and damage. It means that many tens of thousands of people can enjoy this very special countryside without its landscape quality suffering, even though the most popular areas can be overcrowded at the busiest times.

Pressures and conflicts

Has the Dales suffered because of these increased pressures of recreation ?

There have been some quite serious conflicts. Even walkers, whose feet perhaps impose the least damage on a landscape, can in some areas by their sheer numbers cause serious erosion. For example, when walking across soft peat land areas, heavily used routes over peat bog can result in rapidly widening areas of erosion, as people avoid the worst boggy areas other people have created, and erosion spreads until it can be tens of metres wide.

The most extreme example of this process is the Three Peaks Walk, a 24 mile "Challenge" walk from Horton in Ribblesdale over the summits of Pen y Ghent, Whernside and Ingleborough, which in order to qualify for a badge has to be completed in under twelve hours. Not only does this route attract many thousands of individual walkers per year but also many large groups, some of who do the Walk as a challenge to raise money for charity. There is even an annual Three Peaks race for mountain bikers.

Unfortunately much of the Three Peaks Walk crosses extreme boggy terrain where severe erosion has occurred. Over a twenty-year period, what began as an innocent feat of personal endurance in spectacular surroundings developed into a major ecological disaster, with paths up to 100 metres wide in places over deep peat bog which, once the fragile surface is destroyed, cannot be repaired. Many different solutions have been tried, including board walks, netting, chemical solidifiers, but ultimately the best technique has proved to be the oldest – stone flags or causeway stones, used from monastic times onwards. But paving the worst parts of the Three Peaks route has proved a slow and expensive process, requiring the use of helicopters to get suitable stone paving in place.

If feet cause erosion, hooves and tyres are worse. Fortunately levels of horse riding and mountain biking along the byway and bridleway network in the Dales are not yet sufficient to cause too many problems, but the growing fashion for off road vehicles is quite another problem.

Many of the old green lanes, such as Mastiles Lane in Malhamdale or the Craven Way in Ribblesdale, which are such landscape features of the Dales, may be subject to ancient vehicular rights. Originally the right to take a

Cyclists descend Mastiles Lane towards Kilnsey. The surface of much of this ancient route has since suffered severe damage from 4x4 off-road vehicles using it as a sporting challenge. Such activity was prohibited under a Traffic Regulation Order introduced in 2004.

Horse riders on Boss Moor, between Hetton and Bordley. Horse riding in the Dales has hitherto been at a level that has caused few problems, although riders feel there are insufficient bridleways. An official National Trail, the Pennine Bridleway, has recently been designated and passes through much of Ribblesdale. (Colin Raw)

horse and cart along a track, these may date back to medieval times. Use of these lanes has often been claimed by motor cyclists, to the detriment of other users such as walkers, cyclists and horse riders.

However the legal definition of vehicle rights can also include the right to drive a powerful modern 4x4 off-road vehicle. As well as being a contemporary fashion accessory, such vehicles have encouraged a whole new generation of devotees who now target the Dales for their own particular sporting activity. This means taking their vehicles over the wildest, roughest terrain possible to enjoy the challenge of getting out of difficulty and pitting man and machine against that terrain. In so doing, however, enormous physical damage is inflicted on the surface of the green lane, creating deep ruts. The noise and physical presence of such vehicles in perhaps isolated locations can destroy any feeling of peace and tranquillity, the very reason why many people come to enjoy the special environment of a National Park away from urban stress and noise pollution.

The noise, disturbance and damage by off-road vehicles in the Yorkshire Dales is not only the greatest cause of physical damage to the National Park by recreational activity, but creates most complaints by the local community and other users. It also raises a fundamental point endorsed by the Sandford Committee in its seminal 1976 Report on National Parks. This concluded that if and when recreation and conservation are in conflict in a National Parks, then conservation, the protection of the resource, must prevail. This is a sound principle and one that over the first half century of the Yorkshire Dales National Park has largely been endorsed. It is hoped that changing legislation and a toughening of attitude by North Yorkshire County Council, the highway authority, will regulate the situation and help protect the most vulnerable routes where most conflict occurs.

Two walkers, who would then unquestionably have arrived on foot, reach the gates of Grinton Youth Hostel in the 1950s. After massive modernisation this is now a YHA flagship, although other youth hostels in the Dales have been closed. (Lucie Hinson)

Long distance walking - true sustainable tourism

One of the most creative concepts of the 1949 Act was the power for the National Parks Commission, now the Countryside Agency, to create Long Distance Footpaths, now known as National Trails. The first, and still the most famous of these, was the Pennine Way, which runs for 250 miles from Edale in the Peak District, linking Youth Hostels through the South Pennines, the Yorkshire Dales, the North Pennines and Northumberland National Park before reaching Kirk Yetholm on the Scottish Border. The Pennine Way goes though the heart of the Yorkshire Dales, from Gargrave to Malham, Malham Moor, Fountain Fell, Horton in Ribblesdale, Hawes, Thwaite, Keld, Tan Hill

and Stainmoor. Opened in Malham in 1965 by its visionary creator, Tom Stephenson, Secretary of the Ramblers Association and one of the founding fathers of the National Park movement, the Pennine Way enshrined the principles of the long backpacking walk through wild and remote countryside. This was a concept that originated in the Black Forest, Germany, at the turn of the twentieth century, and reached England via the USA when Tom was approached about the idea of a British version of the Appalachian Way.

Though there has been only one other official National Trail in the Yorkshire Dales, the recently designated Pennine Bridleway, several other popular long distance "Regional" routes have been developed. The most popular is perhaps the Dales Way, an 81 mile walk which links Ilkley, at the edge of the West Yorkshire conurbation, with the Lake District. It extends through the heart of the Yorkshire Dales, along Wharfedale via Bolton Abbey, Burnsall, Grassington, Kettlewell Buckden and Langstrothdale, before crossing Cam Fell near the source of the Wharfe and into Dentdale. From Dent the Dales Way continues to Sedbergh, along the Rawthey and Lune, and the low Lakeland foothills via Burneside and Staveley to Bowness on Windermere.

Using Youth Hostel or local bed and breakfast accommodation, both the Pennine Way and the Dales Way enshrine the principle of what is now known as Sustainable Tourism - tourism which inflicts the least damage on the environment, but maximum benefit to the local economy. Walkers, staying at inns, guest houses, youth hostels, camp sites, buying meals, refreshment, services, spend money locally and use local services and produce, thereby helping to sustain the local economy.

The terrible Foot and Mouth epidemic - the second and by far the worse to affect the Yorkshire Dales National Park - which hit the area in 2001 made the whole Dales community recognise the importance of tourism and visitor spend to the upland economy. Tourism now has an equal place to farming in the Dales in terms of wealth generation, and has perhaps an even higher importance in directly and indirectly creating employment in the area. The F&M tragedy also underlined the degree to which urban and rural areas are totally inter-dependent - visitors need the health and spiritual benefits that the National Park can bring, local communities need the visitor spend that bring economic life to the area. It is a complex picture and must even include the many people who move to the Dales on retirement and who are, to a certain degree, permanent tourists in that they bring their income and spend from outside the area into the local economy.

Maintaining the Balance - the challenges ahead

Sustainability is an overused word, but it should reflect the degree to which a particular leisure activity can help maintain the special natural and cultural landscape of the Dales rather than its degradation and destruction. There are thousands of examples in the world where mass, mechanised tourism has destroyed a natural environment, or reduced somewhere very special to something unpleasant and artificial, dominated by traffic, pollution and unsightly development. Sustainable modes of tourism and leisure activity, that is activities such as walking, cycling, horse riding and even angling, can, if they are at the right scale and degree, help maintain what is a careful balance. Challenge walks and rides, motorised sports which have little or no consideration for other people, and other large scale activities, appropriate in a city or urban landscape but not in the fragile environment of a National Park, destroy sustainability and undermine everything a National Park was set up to achieve.

Everyone who loves and cares for the Yorkshire Dales should be grateful for successive generations of National Park officers who, often with extremely limited resources and not always with the political backing they have deserved, have been able to keep at least something approaching that essential balance.

An encouraging feature of the present time is that there is now a new generation of National Park officers with perhaps a clearer and greater understanding of sustainability, a recognition that conservation and recreation are in fact two sides of the same coin; you can't have one without the other. A commitment to a socially inclusive National Park, which means one which is available for all - and not just the most fortunate - to enjoy, is fundamental to National Park purposes. Vital too is the development of the kind of recreational activities which will both respect and appreciate its unique natural environment and at the same time support the local economy.

But the Yorkshire Dales is no island. We live in world of rapid economic and social change, dominated by the twin threats of international terrorism and global warming. We need the Dales as a living reservoir of older, perhaps more permanent values, a reminder of who we were and who we now are, a sense of human continuity. Above all, the Yorkshire Dales can help us understand our own place in the natural world, whose ecological imperatives, ultimately, cannot be ignored. Re-creation in the Yorkshire Dales, in the fullest sense of the word, has never been more important to us, not only at the present time but also for the half century ahead. Hopefully its values will survive well beyond those coming decades to inspire and motivate generations yet to come.

No Wind Farms, Please!

David Bellamy ends this look at the Changing Dales by going back seven thousand rather than just fifty years. Asked to name his favourite place in the Dales, he hedges his bets but is in no doubt that a national treasure must be looked after for the benefit of all future generations.

Choosing a favourite place to live in the Yorkshire Dales National Park is rather like listening to Classic FM and then trying to choose a favourite piece of music. Every time you visit it there's something new to discover. So I am going to hedge or rather drystone wall my bets and luxuriate in my favourite features that make this great slab of landscape so worthy of its status as a National Park. A landscape that is so wonderful and so important that it is regarded as a national treasure looked after for and by the nation for the benefit of all future generations. What greater accolade could there be?

For starters, we must realise that it is not natural, it is all people made and people managed. Take all the people away and it would change out of all recognition. Some seven thousand years ago it would have appeared a very different place. Not that you would have been able to see much because all the views would have been obscured by trees. Thanks to nature's own brand of global warming the whole landscape was then covered with native forest. What is more travel would have been a nightmare! Yes - then the climate was around five degrees warmer than it is today and no one could blame the burning of fossil fuels.

There are of course many small patches of woodland left but none can be called natural. Here I go! - my favourites are in Swaledale. Standing in one of these, sheltering from the rain or the sun, you can almost hear the axes of the first farmers opening up the land with nothing more than chunks of polished stone that had been imported from the Lake District.

People had been there before, hunting and gathering food and fishing the streams and rivers that flowed down through the ancient forests. But thanks to these new Stone Age people the landscape as we now know it began to come into being. Pastures, meadows and fields linked by tracks made living and travelling much easier. Yes - it was these Neolithic farmers and the Bronze and Iron Age people who followed on that added the picture postcard views and the biodiversity to the National Park. Try Wharfedale for starters.

The acid moorlands stretch ahead - home of the grouse. The setting for this painting by Robert Nicholls is Carlton Moor, between Coverdale and Walden.

Heather moor - among the rarest sort of vegetation in the world - gives way to the drystone walls snaking uphill and down dale. This inspiring panorama extends from Harkerside Moor in Swaledale down to Healaugh and back up to Reeth Low Moor.
(Mike Kipling Photography)

For those who believe in global warming, well the latest spell started over fifteen thousand years ago melting the glaciers that then covered the Park and much of Britain. Since then the temperature has gone up and down at irregular intervals causing havoc with the weather and the landscape. There are convenient car parks throughout the Park where you can stop and climb up onto the big rock outcrops (careful as you go!) and, on a winter's day, dream that the Ice Age never came to an end.

Great Shunner Fell - "favourite high spot" - is buzzard country. At least twenty pairs are thought to nest in the Dales but the species is on the Red List of High Conservation Concern. This striking study by Robert Nicholls is set above Oxnop - a matter of minutes to the east for an adult buzzard.

My favourite high spot is Great Shunner Fell. If you have not done that particular slog up the Pennine Way (I always expect to meet Wainwright coming the other way - if only I had!), the limestones with that unique breed the potholers are behind you. The acid moorlands stretch ahead, home of the grouse, the upland gamekeepers and shepherds whose tireless work helps keep the trees at bay and the Park to pay its way.

All that moorland - especially the "squiggiest" bits where even tramping feet cause immense damage - has to be kept in good repair. It is backbreaking work that must be supervised by experts for the heather moor and blanket bog is among the rarest sorts of vegetation in the world. Fortunately there are plenty of volunteers from groups like the National Trust and the British Trust for Conservation Volunteers to help them.

From the top, what a spectacle! There they are, those drystone walls snaking up hill and back down into those dales - north, south, east and west - and always there to provide shelter from the wind and a warm back rest when the sun has been shining. Wow! - what better welcome could there be than that in the villages in the Yorkshire Dales?

No - I am not even going to dare to choose a favourite village but will ask myself a rhetorical question. How did the planners get it so right in those horse-drawn days? Perhaps it was that there were no real planners - just locals who fitted the landscape like the landscape fitted them.

Then of course there's always a church or chapel, where you can get down on your knees and say thank you - and please don't even consider letting those silver satanic mills they have the audacity to call wind farms mar the views from this amazing place.

Part 3

The Dales Today

Daffodils bursting into bloom are a sure sign that winter is almost past and spring is just round the corner. This display is in front of the packhorse bridge at Linton in Wharfedale, widely regarded as one of the most attractive villages in the whole of the Dales. (Geoff Lund)

Through the Year

This third part of the book begins with a pictorial look at the Yorkshire Dales of today through the four seasons. It does so not just in conventional terms but through the eyes of both photographers and artists striving to capture this land of fickle light and fleeting colour in all its many moods. Collectively they depict not just mountains and dales but also such facets as sheep and swallows, heather and hawthorns, barns and bridges.

Spring in the Dales sees a myriad of greens burst forth in all directions, creating a hauntingly beautiful backcloth for wild flowers and new-born lambs. By mid-May a Dales river is a shade of quite extraordinary subtlety reflecting the tender young foliage on either bank. High summer can be a dense and all-pervading green, but fast forward to an autumn afternoon and the chances are high of being enraptured by a sun-dappled patchwork of peat-stained becks, limestone scree and all the colours of a Dales fellside in the evening of the year. Come the depths of winter and a new dimension is provided by the intense low-level light, picking out to superb effect the dry stone walls and remains of ancient field systems.

The Dales truly offers riches through the year.

The call of the curlew and the bleating of lambs herald the return of life to the "tops" of the Dales after the quiet of winter. These ewes and their hardy followers are above Stainforth, with the unmistakable profile of Penyghent in the background.

(Mike Kipling Photography)

A hawthorn tree, seemingly growing out of nothing in the joints of a limestone pavement, has become almost a trademark of the Yorkshire Dales, widely used in promotional literature. Hannah Chesterman's painting (opposite) depicts a tree on the extensive range of pavements that stretches north from Grassington. A stunted hawthorn in spring has a special magic, as shown on Southerscales Nature Reserve, near Ingleborough. (above - Granville Harris)

The glory of Wensleydale.

(Above) *Generations of dalesfolk have looked forward to the annual return of the swallows, which are the most wonderful of birds to watch in flight. Robert Nicholls painted this pair on the River Ure with Askrigg in the distance.*

(Opposite, top) *This study of sheep above Hawes, with Stags Fell on the skyline, is also by Robert Nicholls.*

(Lower) *Panorama looking downdale from a meadow near Askrigg with Lady Hill - noted for its crown of trees - visible in the distance.* Painting by Judith Bromley.

The show season brings a flourish to high summer in the Dales.

(Above) *Mule, Jacob, Suffolk and Texel sheep at Kilnsey Show. It is a scorching hot August day but already the long shadows of Kilnsey Crag are creeping towards the showfield. Compare this picture with those on pages 64 and 65.* (Geoffrey Lund)

(Opposite,top) *Vintage tractors - including this red beast by David Brown - enter the ring at Malham Show.*

(Lower) *Sheep pens at Reeth Show attract much critical opinion from the local farming community.* (John Potter - 2)

As summer turns into autumn, the colour content of the Dales landscape becomes ever more spectacular. (Above) *Stainforth packhorse bridge near Settle, with fallen leaves speckling the still waters of the Ribble.* (Granville Harris) (Opposite, top) *A gathering storm over Bolton Priory bathes the River Wharfe in fleeting light - a noted feature of the Dales.* (Colin Raw) (Lower) *Nature's "special effects" can also inspire artists, as was clearly the case when Lawrence Roy Wilson painted Kilnsey Crag from the Trout Farm.*

Autumn splendour in Wharfedale at Barden bridge, unaltered since it was rebuilt in 1659. (Geoff Lund)

Barden bridge looking up-river, depicted by artist Hannah Chesterman and photographer Colin Raw from precisely the same vantage point.

Living on the edge of the Dales, the artist Kitty North is constantly surprised by the swiftness of changes in the weather: "The light fails as the clouds swarm in, the blue sky fades dismally and even the grass looks grey." She strives to captures the moods of mountain, moor and dale in her work as well as the seas of seasonal colour and the immensity of the scene. A recent series of paintings has focussed on "the distinctive scattering of hill farms and stone barns throughout the landscape".
(Above) *Golden Day.*
(Opposite, top) *Nature's Impression.*
(Lower) *Rainstorm.*

Although climate changes mean that the spectacle is becoming less common, the two pairs of photographs on these pages illustrate just how dramatic can be the transition from autumn to winter. (This page) *Embsay Reservoir and Crag, near Skipton.* (Colin Raw - 2)

Castle Farm and Fremington Edge, Arkengarthdale. A dusting of snow highlights many features of the landscape not immediately obvious in the early autumn picture.
(Mike Kipling Photography - 2)

Animals in the snow.

(Above) *A gnarled tree trunk precariously resting on a wall head frames a group of sheep above Kettlewell.* (Geoff Lund)
(Opposite) *Robert Nicholls' paintings of sheep near the Ure and a fox among deep drifts both have Ellerkin, the fell on the north side of Wensleydale near Askrigg, as their background.*

Deep snow makes two of the famous Three Peaks of Yorkshire seem even more impressive. Few readers of this book should need to have them identified, but the top picture is of Ingleborough and the lower one of Penyghent. (Colin Raw - 2)

Looking Ahead

Dales children don't want the Yorkshire Dales to change. That much is abundantly clear from their prose, poems and paintings that form the final section of this book. They love their meadows, moors, sheep and anything to do with farming.

Adults reached a similar conclusion back in 1989 when the National Park embarked on a pioneering project to determine what sort of future landscape local people and visitors wished to see. Based on interviews with a whole gamut of interest groups, various options were drawn up and translated into paintings by local artist Hannah Chesterman (whose work is also featured in this book). At one extreme was a wilderness future with farming abandoned, or the land deliberately set aside to go back to nature, and with little local employment except in catering for those on walking and wildlife holidays. At the other was an option whereby further incentives were given to farmers without regard to conservation, with the erection of ugly farm buildings and the disappearance of walls, field barns and the remaining flower-rich meadows. Much more attractive was a vision of a largely unchanged landscape with well-maintained walls and barns, flower-filled meadows stretching across the valleys to distant heather moors and with rather more broad-leaved trees. Perhaps not surprisingly this was the option favoured by the majority of respondents, who made it clear that they deeply valued the characteristic Dales scene. They felt that the walls and barns helped to make the area a jewel in the nation's crown and wanted to keep such "treasures" for future generations to enjoy.

So fifteen years on, what are the prospects? Viewed purely as a piece of landscape, the answer is probably as good as can be expected. The threats once posed by quarrying and afforestation have receded, but they have been replaced by factors utterly outside the control of planners or anyone else. Globalisation and the growth of the world economy could lead to the abandonment of agricultural subsidies and tariffs, while the prospect of an acute water shortage due to global warming may not be as remote a threat as some imagine. In both cases the consequences for the Dales would be devastating.

It is when people are brought into the equation that it gets much more complicated. On the face of it we have in the words of Harold Macmillan never had it so good. The 2001 census revealed that unemployment in the Dales is a tiny 1.5 per cent - the lowest in any National Park - with the long-term unemployed a minute 0.32 per cent. The number owning their own homes is 74 per cent, a figure only exceeded by the Peak District. Only 12 per cent of households do not have their own car, a lower statistic than any other Park except remote Northumberland.

Yet behind the figures all is not quite so rosy. Two key issues currently emerge from any study of the Dales and have been brought into sharp focus on the preceding pages. One is that unless the current housing crisis can be solved in the very near future, young people are going to be forced to leave the area in droves. The other is that farming is poised on the edge of a precipice and, if it collapses, then all that is held most dear in the Dales will collapse with it.

Putting the two together creates the prospect of a soulless ghetto of the rich, divorced from reality and inhabited largely by second homers and the privileged. Their relative wealth and clout, buoyed by tourism and high property prices, will enable the Dales to remain a scenic wonderland but the thriving local community - rich in character, custom and tradition - will have gone.

Doug Macleod, a farmer living at the head of Littondale, has summed up the present frustration: "Current policy is not preserving the life of the Dales, it is killing it off by turning the place into a museum. No one milks cows here in Littondale any more and there are - I hear - now more lawyers than working farmers in the dale. Dales farming is about to be eradicated as surely as a greengrocer's shop when a new supermarket opens up. Farming families must diversify if they are to stay in the Dales. To do so they don't need any initiatives, seminars, regeneration schemes or 'workers' paid to talk to other bureaucrats. They need good roads and services, modern communications and - above all - planners who recognise that people need buildings from which they can earn a living."

In the robust cut and thrust of Dales politics, planners certainly can't complain that they don't receive critical feedback! Nor is there any shortage of policy. It descends from on high like confetti as government departments issue directives on everything from sustainable development to renewable energy and biodiversity to the built environment. The National Park's new draft Local Plan, designed to shape all future planning proposals, weighs in at 2.4 kilograms and contains 557 clauses and 95 policy statements.

Yet it wasn't policy that created the Yorkshire Dales landscape and character that seemingly everyone wishes to endure. It was, as David Bellamy perceptively comments on page 100, locals who fitted the landscape like the landscape fitted them. The masons of old possessed an innate skill and a spark of fire that once made the humblest barn a thing of beauty. They were also at one with local needs and materials, with the result that a recognisably different style of building evolved in each dale. Policy tends to be a great leveller with the result that not only do new buildings lack such variation, but also it is doubtful if any will henceforth be sufficiently inspirational to receive "listing" status for their architectural importance. This is not just a criticism of planners but also a reflection on mankind and the slap-dash nature of modern society. One has only to look at Nidderdale, the portion of the Dales excluded from the National Park, to see that other areas have fared much worse.

So what can be done to make policy a servant rather than a slave and thus help to solve at least some of the fundamental problems centred round farming and housing? One difficulty is that policy comes from a raft of different bodies and they don't always appear to ensure that it is coherent by talking to one another. It is a bit like the post-privatisation railway, where anything remotely at fault is blamed on another company or contractor. Such an approach cuts no ice with an aggrieved Dales farmer or a young person about to be compelled to leave the area to seek a roof over his head. They simply want action - and are not interested in the niceties of whether this is instigated by central government, the National Park or the district council.

This situation is being addressed by District Council Local Strategic Partnerships, a title that smacks of bureaucracy at its worst but in fact embraces real concerns and hopes. Their underlying message is that the prime conservation and visitor purposes of a National Park are intimately dependent on the continuing contribution of the local communities. Put at its simplest, they aim to avoid "unpleasantly divisive argument" about national versus local interest and instead get the myriad of different parties to agree a course of action.

In the meantime, there is scant recognition at government level that any problems exist. Margaret Beckett, Secretary of State for Rural Affairs, stated early in 2004 that "taken as a whole, the quality of life for those living in rural areas is better on a number of key indicators than their urban counterparts". Descending to regional level, more hope is offered by Yorkshire Forward's Rural Renaissance project, which hinges round the belief that a thriving economy will only be achieved if people can work as well as live in the countryside. It proposes to create better job opportunities in rural locations by providing high-quality premises designed to attract equally high-quality businesses. Like so much else, it will not happen overnight.

Happily, there are developments at local level on the housing front. Housing Association schemes have been completed in several locations including Hawes, Askrigg, Reeth, West Burton, Litton and Kilnsey. The most recent has been at Kettlewell, where there were fourteen applicants for the five homes. One of the successful five was James Bowdin, a dry stone waller married with two young children, who had been forced to spend the previous five years living away from the village because of the lack of any affordable property. He now found himself paying a rent of £278 per month compared with what would otherwise have been around £550.

The National Park is developing new policies that will allow the building of up to seven hundred new houses, largely in the key centres of Grassington, Hawes, Reeth and Sedbergh with occupancy restricted to local families. More controversially, there are also proposals to allow barns to be converted into houses - again for local people - in many isolated settlements. Finally, high hopes have been expressed for a "Half a House" plan, whereby investors - and especially those with a deep love of the Dales - put money into a shared equity scheme. Those wanting a home in the area buy part of a house and have the option to purchase more of the property when they can afford it. When the house is sold on the open market the equity is split proportionately.

On the farming front, little in the long history of agriculture in the Dales has ever happened with undue

Signpost to the future? Enjoyment of the Dales will hopefully continue to grow at a level that is manageable. This footpath from the north bank of the Swale to Healaugh village is clearly well used. Even if the two walkers are not quite obeying the exhortation on the sign to keep in single file, the buttercup meadow is in good shape. Modern agricultural buildings in the background indicate that this is still a living village- and long may it remain so. (Mike Kipling Photography)

haste. Yet there are encouraging signs of progress in tackling some of the issues outlined in the farming chapter. A new abattoir has been built at Bainbridge enabling prime stock to be slaughtered locally and spared a journey across half of Europe as a mere commodity. A similar venture at Skipton means that much of the wholesome produce of the Dales can be sold with its origins clearly identified. Much has been achieved despite reckless competition by supermarkets determined to drive all others to the wall.

Julia Horner, a National Trust tenant farmer in Upper Wharfedale, has eloquently summed up the importance of these ventures: "Such recognition of identity of origin and nature of production has to be the salvation of the small family farm - and the Dales. Foot and Mouth showed very clearly that agriculture and tourism are inextricably linked. But it's the functionality of the countryside, its ingenuity and initiative, which must come first. A countryside cannot exist just to sustain visitors. If it tries to do that, there will be no room to develop the essence of identity which will stagnate, forever returning to countryside clichés that are naff, tawdry and twee. Politicians come and go, but at the end of the day we will only survive if their policies can be made to add up. I don't know a more resourceful, gritty and hard-working workforce who are as determined and tenacious as the thymes that cling to these hills, to remain to weather the storm, so that the life, culture, tradition and good food of the Dales will survive and be enjoyed for generations to come."

It is difficult to conceive any better sentiments - optimistic and yet realistic - on which to end a chapter that looks ahead to the future of the Yorkshire Dales.

From Four to Eleven
The New Generation of Dalesfolk

What expectations do children in the Dales have of the area in which they live? In a bid to do some crystal ball gazing, we invited the twenty-seven Primary Schools within or on the edge of the National Park to submit material for this book. We asked children to depict in prose, poetry, paintings or drawings what they most liked – or least liked – about the Dales. More than half the schools responded with a total of almost five hundred submissions. From them we have selected the fifty that appear on the following pages, with the child's name, age and school being given in each case.

Children are naturally optimistic but the overwhelming impression is of a group of youngsters aware that there is more to life than TV and truly appreciative of the countryside in which they live. The prose and poems wax lyrical on colourful meadows, heather-covered moors, swirling waterfalls, winding paths in the woods and acres of space. Even brainless pheasants, pubs and Dales ice cream find their place.

Rivers and becks, high peaks and drystone walls all feature in the paintings and drawings. But it is both reassuring and thought provoking that the farming scene still dominates. There are lots of tractors, many hay bales, a few cattle and an almost overwhelming number of sheep. One drawing (page 137 – lower) makes careful use of perspective to feature over a hundred of them.

Dales children are both perceptive and talented. The painting on page 137 (top right) is an inspirational vision of the landscape. That of "Haytime" (page 136 – top) makes outstanding use of different shades of yellow, although its down-to-earth creator comments: "I don't like haytime because you get too hot lifting the bales which itches your skin."

Likes vastly outnumber dislikes, but rain, mud, litter, campers and even "bad smells from muckspreading" all receive their share of criticism. Regret that dad is too busy on the farm is occasionally evident. More worrying is a strong anti-tourist sentiment that runs through a surprising number of contributions. Here is a new generation inheriting the prejudices of the past but facing a future where the old ways cannot continue. In another fifty years some of its members may look back, just as this book has done. Hopefully, they will see tourism as a vital part of prosperity in the Dales – prosperity in which they and their children can share.

Henry Giles (4), Kettlewell.

The Moors

Rabbits jumping
Foxes prowling
Ducks paddling
Pheasants pecking
Dad game keeping
Colourful moors.

The Yorkshire Dales

I can see lambs being born
I can see birds singing in the trees
I can see the countryside all around us
I can see beautiful flowers
I can see sheep grazing in the grass
The Dale is a wonderful place.

(Top, left) *Alice Lucy Rackham (5), Kettlewell.*
(Top, right) *Tom Entwistle (5), Askrigg.*
(Centre) *Lily Orrell (6), Kirkby Malham.*
(Lower) *"Where I Live", Thomas Richardson (6), Kirkby Malham.*

(Opposite, top) *Marian Porter (6), Reeth (who was clearly inspired by the new suspension bridge over the River Swale).*
(Lower) *"Malham Tarn", Martha Pickles (6), Kirkby Malham.*

(This page, top) *Thomas Short (7), Reeth (a drawing that must surely depict the centre of Reeth village).*
(Lower, left) *Richard Breen (7), Grassington.*
(Lower, right) *Curtis Lee Oversby (7), Kettlewell.*

The river in summer

I love the river it's so much fun, if
I could I'd play there all day long.
I like the sound of the water splashing
against small rocks. I find the sand
in between my toes soothing. It is a
brilliant place to have lovely picnics
without getting too much sand in your
food. And the nature smells beautiful
and the view from the bridge is very
pretty. There are sometimes crayfish
so watch out. They normally hide
under the rocks and you can take the
crayfish home and eat them.

Two lambs in a pen

The wildlife

The good thing about the Yorkshire dales is that there is a lot of wildlife. The wildlife is good.

The other good thing about the yorkshire dales is we don't get polution or Graffitti.

Lambing time

Lambing time is nice because I love to see the lambs skipping around. When you go on the motorbike and make sure every lamb has a mum.

I Do not like the litter. That does not go in the bins.

I like the yorkshire dales because we do not have to just walk or run on pavements like in citys we can walk in the country side

I like the views from the windows. I like the river.

(Opposite, top) *William Wildman (7), Kirkby Malham*
(Lower) *Katy Whyte (8), Burnsall.*

(This page, top and centre) *"Kilnsey Crag" - drawing and prose by Ben Rymer (8), Grassington.*
(Below) *"On the Farm" - drawing and prose by John Stubbs (8), Arkengarthdale.*

Kilnsey Crag

Kilnsey Crag is where people climb up a big cliff that has trees on it. It is made out of rock, stone and grass. Rabbits run up and down Kilnsey Crag. It has trees on it. They are called Ash trees.

When you get to the top of Kilnsey Crag, the bottom is really small from the top. On Kilnsey Crag there is hang over. It has a dry stone wall around it and a gate to get in. Sometimes there are sheep in the field, and birds that go on top of Kilnsey Crag sing nearly all day long.

The Yorkshire Dales

My favourite time of year is lambing time, Because I like to see the lambs hopping and bouncing up and down the fields and the calves galloping into the sun as they eat grass. My mum and dad are so busy they have not much time for me but I still help on the farm. But it's worth it because I get to see first all the little lambs being bottle fed.

Advice from Emily

What I most like about living in the Yorkshire Dales is what goes on there. All the things that are in the Yorkshire Dales can be used for something. Like the hills can be used for walking your dog.

The caves are good for exploring and also for finding things. But you must beware that you don't slip because caves sometimes have a little bit of water in. If I were you I would take some equipment like a torch or a drink and snack.

Castleberg is a big hill with lots of paths. They added a new path called the Tot Lord trail. On the new path you are allowed to go bird watching and some of them are rare. Castleberg is near my house and is one of my favourite walks ever.

There are quite a lot of places to go mountain climbing, but you have to be fully equipped to go as it can be quite dangerous. You have to find a good climbing mountain and it has to be quite high too.

That's why I love living in the Yorkshire Dales!

Grass Woods

My favourite place in the Yorkshire Dales is Grass Woods. Because you can smell the beautiful scent of flowers. And you can find beech trees, sycamore trees and many more. But what I don't like is camps, they leave all kinds of litter. If animals eat it they will die. And if you go to the middle you have a lovely view.

The Yorkshire Dales

In the Yorkshire Dales...
Wear a hood
Falling rain
Splattering mud

In the Yorkshire Dales...
Mossy trees
Broad branches
Falling leaves

In the Yorkshire Dales...
Tourists come
With caravans
All day long

In the Yorkshire Dales...
Mountains high
Birds are soaring
Across the sky

In the Yorkshire Dales...
Hedgehogs crawl
Beetles scuttle
Along the wall

In the Yorkshire Dales..
Day is done
Over the viaduct
With setting sun

(This page, top left) *Lucy Lundberg (8), Arkengarthdale.*
(Top right) *Michael Moon (8), Long Preston.*
(Centre) *Emily Preston (8), Settle.*
(Lower) *Mollie Darwin (8), Grassington.*

(Opposite, top) *Conor Rigby (8), Settle.*
(Lower) *"Over the hills and far away", Alex Cardwell (9), Long Preston (who must surely have been hugely impressed by Ribblehead viaduct).*

Yorkshire is The Best

- It's a wonderful place to come on holiday but if you live here its like a holiday forever.
- It's a wonderful scene especially Pheny-Ghent.
- There's pubs and fields to play in.
- There's allsorts of animals.
- You'll meet lots of friends to meet
- In spring all the birds sing.

I ♡ THE YORKSHIRE DALES!

You must come to the Yorkshire Dales because there are beautiful views to see.

There are beautiful flowers in the fields.

In Swaledale there are lots of patch works of dry stone walls.

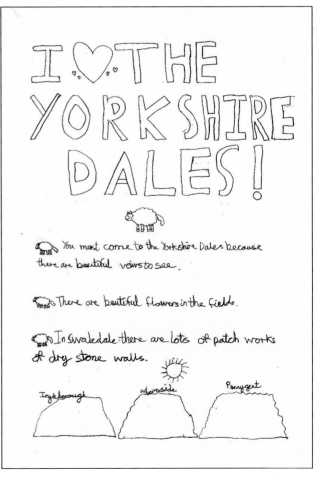

(Opposite, top) *Isabella Pratt (9), Askrigg (could it be the high bridge at Aysgarth Falls?)*
(Lower, left) *Bill Hallworth (9), Horton in Ribblesdale.*
(Lower, right) *Jessica Lambert (9), Horton in Ribblesdale.*

(This page, top) *Claire Hargreaves (9), Threshfield.*
(Below, left) *Monica Yeadon (9), Threshfield.*
(Below, right) *John Mark (9), Long Preston.*

*What I don't like about
living in the National Park*

*First there's heavy rain,
Added to all the tourists,
Then there's traffic jams,
Litter and bad smells
from muckspreading.
Speeding motor cycles and crashes.
Dead pheasants on the road and mud.*

What I like about the Yorkshire Dales

I like the roads of the Yorkshire dales
because of the bends and turns,
I think the walls of the Yorkshire dales
because of the colours and shades,
I like the trees of the Yorkshire dales
because of the greens and reds,
I believe the plants of the Yorkshire
dales because of the pinks and blues,
I like the grass of the Yorkshire dales
because of the movement and sway,
I like the rivers of the Yorkshire dales
because of the blues and greens,
But the best thing of all about the
Yorkshire dales is the scenery and the
views.

The Yorkshire Dales

Misty Mountains ride the sky,
Thick green forests travel by,
Thundery rivers crash down the hill,
Everyone's quiet, animals still.

Steep winding paths, cloaked in dust,
Bits of rock, looking like crust,
Muddy grass here and there,
Is something more beautiful, then where?

The Yorkshire Dales

The Yorkshire Dales National Park is a beautiful and safe place to live. There are monstrous hills, lots of grassy green fields and sparkling, swirling waterfalls trickling down into calm still pools. Children run and play, climbing trees and swimming in cool streams. In the winter watch the icy white snow falling past the playhouse. Run outside and pull out your sledge. When you go whizzing down the steep, snowy hills look at the stunning view and imagine … why would you want to be anywhere else?

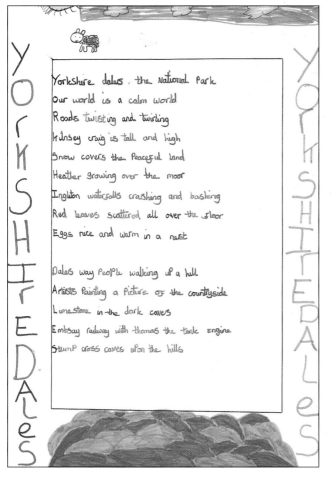

Yorkshire Dales

Yorkshire dales, the National Park
Our world is a calm world
Roads twisting and twirling
Kilnsey craig is tall and high
Snow covers the peaceful land
Heather growing over the moor
Ingleton waterfalls crashing and bashing
Red leaves scattered all over the floor
Eggs nice and warm in a nest

Dales way people walking up a hill
Artists painting a picture of the countryside
Limestone in the dark caves
Embsay railway with thomas the tank engine
Stump cross caves upon the hills

Just Free

Slowly, slowly the rabbit moves.
No dusty fumes, No screeching sounds.
Just free, Just free.

Hoppity, Hoppity goes the bright green frog,
Swimming free, Swimming free,
Goes the bright green frog.

Look at me, Look at me,
Dancing free, Dancing free,
Just look at me.

The dazzling hills, the slopey countryside,
Sparkling fields with glittering flowers,
Glowing pinetrees in the night,
Spinning lambs with a gorgeous sight,
What more could a child want
            Free! Free! Free!

(Opposite, top) *Jake Lockwood (9), Threshfield.*
(Centre, right) *Alice Kelly (9), Cracoe.*
(Lower, left) *Alex Moffat (9), Grassington.*
(Lower, right) *Katherine Ellison (9), Askrigg.*

(This page, top left) *Sophie Boreham (9), Gargrave.*
(Top, right) *Hannah Hughes (9), Arkengarthdale.*
(Below) *Alice Hargraves (9), Burnsall (who has shown the school and riverside path in the correct position for this village).*

What I like about the Yorkshire Dales

I like the way the trees blow in the strong wind. I like living here because it's so relaxing. There are good places to go walking and to keep fit.

The one bad thing about living in Reeth is all the mud when it rains. It makes it go like melted ice cream.

Also I like living here because if you want to go to Richmond, or Leyburn on a Friday, there are buses passing through every so often.

Another good thing about living in Reeth are the shops where you can buy sweets. There's an ice-cream parlour where we can get ice creams on a hot summer's day.

There's a car park as well and if you ever get bored then you can just go the park.

If you get hurt there then you can just go to the doctors which is right next to the park.

There's a lot of rivers in Reeth and I like going fishing in them in the summer.

Another thing I don't like about Reeth is in the summer when all of the tourists come because it doesn't make Reeth feel so homely like it usually does.

I really like living in Reeth and I don't really ever want to leave because I've been here nearly all my life and this is my home.

Some of my family live here and if I move I won't be able to see them as much as I do now.

(Opposite, top)   "Haytime", Carol Whitehead (10), Gunnerside (see page 124).
(Lower) Robert Jaune (10), Askrigg (it's clearly Bolton Castle).

(This page, top left) Kelly Jones (10), Reeth.
(Top, right) Rachel Metcalf (10), Long Preston.
(Lower) Ben Parkinson (10), Burnsall.

(Above)   *Jasmine Horrocks (10), Grassington (who has managed to include all sorts of activities in what must be the Square).*
(Below, left) *Three contributions from Threshfield.*
(Below, right) *Annabel Pope (10), Kettlewell.*

My favourite place is Hawkswick village. I like it because there are horses and my house is there. My garden is the best place for peace and quiet – and there are no tourists.
Harry Ecclesall (10)

The River Wharfe is my favourite part of the National Park. I like the scenery best. Another thing special about it is all the wildlife. In the summer it is especially good because there are lots of people you can play with. It's a great place to have fun!
Daniel Coverdale (10)

I want to tell you why I really like Foxup. It is very quiet and not many people live there. An important part of this special place is that there are very few tourists, although there is lots of wildlife and beautiful scenery to enjoy. It is a wonderful place to relax in.
Sophie Devlin (10)

What I like about the Yorkshire dales

Come and stroll through Grasswoods crunching dead leaves of autumn

Come and taste the fresh air and let it twist through you like a cascading stream.

Come and hear the harsh cry of the pheasants fluttering around brainlessly in every direction up down and all around.

But before your day ends sit on a bench and let the dales soak into your mind.

(Above) *Benjamin Hall (11), Gunnerside.*
(Below, left) *Sam Giles (11), Kettlewell.*
(Below, right) *Charlotte Clarke (11), Threshfield*

Use your Senses in the Dales

Feel the fresh air
like water flowing in your lungs.
Hear new-born lambs
bleating till late on at night.
Smell the fresh hay just cut.
Taste a bowl of smooth Dales ice-cream.
See the long colourful meadows
with butterflies like candle flames
flickering in the breeze.
So come and use your senses
you will love the Dales.

What I like most about the Yorkshire Dales.

Climbing up the steep rocky crags in the breeze of the
summer air,
Bird spotting behind a tree looking for a bird
that is new and rare,
The Primroses in the fields represent the coming of
Spring,
In the quiet of the woods and by the stream is where
the birds sing, This is what I like best.

Hiking up the hills in the Yorkshire Dales with my
family and my friends,
Watching the river flowing to and fro and twisting
around the bends,
Seeing the wild life scamper and scuttle along the well
worn track,
Eventually the day is over and I've been on a journey
there and back, this is what I like best.

The Yorkshire Dales

Winding paths in the woods
Very high crags for you to climb,
Lots of things to do and lots of time,
Water and wildlife have their own space too.

Moors have acres of space,
Lots of winding, deep, mysterious caves,
Valleys have a big deep drop to the village below.

Lots of lovely trees and hills,
New-born lambs jumping in the sun,
Having lots and lots of fun,
And also there are some great sights.

As the day comes to an end,
And the limestone contrasts with the darkness,
The artists ready for another day of painting,
And the Yorkshire Dales has closed for the night.

(Above) *Matthew Geldard (11), Grassington*
(Left) *We revert back to the nine-year-old age group for a poem that ends "And the Yorkshire Dales has closed for the night". Written by William Smith of Long Preston school, it forms the appropriate final words for this book.*

Subscribers

Mr & Mrs H N Acaster
B Acres
Pat Adamson
Roz Agar
Robin Parker Airey
Marcia Allass
John Allen
M & K Allen
Audrey Allison
Mrs M A Alnwick
Jean V Andrews
Kiki Angelrath
D A Ansbro
Robert Arbury
Jean Archer
W A Arden
Douglas Armitage
Dorothy Arnott
Anni Arthur
D S Ashbridge
Mr K Aston
Mark & Delia Atkin
Mrs B E Atkinson
Jeanne M Austin
Gordon Avill

Marguerite Babcock
Jean Bagshaw
John D Bailey
David A Baker
Marjorie Baker
Alan David Balme
Mrs Eileen Bannister
Barbara
George T Bargh
Annie Barker
C R Barker
Mrs J Barker
J S Barker
A R & E Barnard
Mr A Barnes
Marjorie A Barnes
C & E M Barraclough
J Barron
Barbara Bartram
Tim Baslington

Jeff Bastow
H Bates
W Tunstall Bates
Andrew Battye
Mr W A Baugh
Sam Beachell
Margaret Bean
Peter Beaumont
Sue Beaumont
E Beevers
Derek Bell
Mary Bell
Tony Bell
Ruth Benn
To Ben Bennett
Nina Benson
Roger H Benson
Caroline Bentley
Muriel and Bernard Berman
Heather Berry
Martyn Berry
Peter Berry
S Berry
Mr T Best
Mrs Joyce M Billington
Arthur Bilsborough
J S Black
S A Blakey
Wm. Neville Blakey
Mrs F G Bland
M I Bleasdale
Desmond Booker
Mr E Booker
Mr J K Booth
L J Booth
Nesta Bottomley
R R Bowden
Eric Bowen
G P Bower
J Bowie
R Bowman
Mrs Sheila Boyes
Mr H J Bradley
Mr & Mrs K Bradley
W H & P Bradley
B Braithwaite-Exley

Reverend Patrick Branagan
C H Brears
Everild Breen
E Brierley
Frank Brimmell
Jill Britland
David Broadbent
Arthur Broadhead
Denis Brockbank
Derek N Broderick
Tony Brook
Patricia Brookes
Y A L Brooksbank
Roely & Alan Broome
A F Brown
Tony Brown
Tony Bryan
David Bubis
Arthur Rowley Buck
Peter G Buckland
Mr R H Buckle
Richard Bull
Tony Bunn
Jane Burdett
Mr & Mrs K Burnett
A T Burnhill
Mr B Burton - Ilkley
Muriel Busfield
C Butler
Winston Butler
David Butterworth
Robert C Bygott
Mrs Brenda Byrnes

D Cairns
Chris Calvert
Mr & Mrs G Cameron
Mr P C Campbell
Kitty Carroll
Margaret C Carter
Maureen Carter
Yvonne & Michael Carter
A J & S Casey
Miss L Catterick
Mr & Mrs M Catterick
Mrs M Chalmers

Mrs Chambers
Bob Chapman
Mr M Charlesworth
B J Charlton
Albert Cheesebrough
Jennifer Chester
Anthony Chisenhale-Marsh
Christine Chisholm
Mrs K M Clapham
Mr & Mrs J D Clark
Prof. Ann Clarke
Mrs D J Clarke
Jean M Clarke
Mr J N Clarkson - Skipton
Mr N J Clarkson - Sheffield
Maureen Clayton
Richard Clayton
Jean Clegg
Margaret Clements
Paula Clements
Cynthia Clifton
Trevor Clough
Richard Coates
H Cobb
Joyce M Cochrane
J Cockerham
Michael Cockerham
Sheila Cockerill
Margaret Codling
Chris Coleman
David Coles
John Collett
John Collins
Mr S R Collins
Mrs Ruth Cook
Colin Cooke
Jennifer Cooke
James E Corden
Mrs Joyce M Cordingley
Jean C Corlett
Patricia A Costen
Lynn Cowlard
Karen Cowley
Andrew D Cox
Mr W G J Cox
C Crabtree

V A Cranston

Mr C Creasey

Mr & Mrs S R L Crebbin

H Crockett

Mr I D Cromack

Val Crompton

Margaret Crowther

J P Curry

Audrey Cussons

Mrs D Cussons

Michael John Cuttle

Denis G Dale

Mrs Lois Darnley

Richard Davey

Judy Davies

P R Davies

Ian Daws

Eric Dean

Denis & Stella

Jeffrey Denton

Mr E S Dickinson

Mrs B Dixon

Mrs P Dodds

Miss Anna Doody

Dr Ian Dormor

Lilian and Trevor Dorsey

Dowling Family

Sid Drake

M R Drinkell

J Driscoll

Rita D Driver

Philip Dronfield

Claire Duffield

Graham F Duffin

Elizabeth Dunhill

F Durance

Edith Durham

Julie Durham

Chris Durrans

Irene Durrans

Emma Dyson

Barbara Eacott

John Earless

Philip Eastwood

Mrs E W Edmondson

Mrs M Edmondson

David Edward

Judy Eland

Charles & Sue Ellis

Mrs L G Ellwood

J B Emmett

Kate Empsall

C P Ensor

Tim Evison

W Raymond Ewbank

Janet Fairs

Janet Farr

Mr & Mrs J Fawcett

Enid Ferriman

Brian Field

John Finney

Debbie and Robert Firth

Mary and Joe Firth

Nell Firth

Mr & Mrs R Fish

Alan Fisher

S P Fisher

Mr John Forster

D J Foster

J W Foster

Sue Foster

Mary G Fowler

Ann Fox

Eileen and David Fox

G A Fox

J Fox

M Fox

Beth Frank (nee King)

H Fraser

J A Fuller

G H Fulstow

John and Jean Gabriel

Jonathan M G Gardner

Tim Gardner

Barry George

Colin Gibbs

David Gibson

Edgar Gilberthorpe

Colin Gilks

H M Glenn

William Goddard

Ian Goldthorpe

Vera Joyce Good

C J Gostridge

Gill & Geoff Goulding

Clive Gray

David and Margaret Gray

Hilda Gray

Catherine Green

Richard G Green

S T Green

K Gregory

K C W Griggs

Gillian Haigh

Mrs Hall

Mr Alan Hall

Alan D Hall

Andrew M Hall

Robert James Hall

Joan Hallam

Kenneth Phipps Hammill

J A Hanslow

Mr & Mrs Duncon Hare

Florence Hargreaves

P Hargreaves

Glenn C Harland

Mark A Harland

Patrick Harlington

John & Norah Harran

Mrs Lynn Harris

Margaret Harris

Harry & Margaret Harrison

Harry

Dick Hartley

Irene Hate

N S Hatto

F Hay

Adrian Heaton

John Helliwell

Maurice Stanley Heppenstall

Susan Hepton

C N Hepworth

Margaret Hepworth

Craig (Rigsby) Higgins

Misses K & D Hilliar

Trevor Hinchliffe

John C Hird

Dorothy & Brian Hirst

J M Hirst

Mr Robert Hirst

Mr J Hodgson

Mrs Barbara Hogg

Yvonne Hogg

Lawrence Holden

J Holdsworth

H Holmes

John E Holmes

Rene Holmes

Marjory Holt

Rodney W Holt

Ann Holubecki

Fiona and David Hoole

John Hooper

Tony Hopkins

Joshua L Hopkinson

Josephine Hopper

C & E Hopwood

D Horne

Mr J D Hornsby

John and Cynthia Howard

Michael B Howard

Mrs J Howard

Dorothy Hoyle

Jean Mary Hoyle

Rev`d & Mrs A G Hudson

Ruth B Hudson

Tony Hudson

Cyril Hulley

David & Mary Hunt

Mr G A Hunt

Miss Kathleen M Hunt

Mr A G Hutchinson

Bob Hutchinson

Mrs Janet Hutchinson

W N Hutchinson

Mr & Mrs J R Hutton

David Ilett

Alan Inder

M Ingham

M Ireson

Mrs Freda Jackson

Peter Jackson

Reg Jackson

A Jamieson

Chris Jarvis

H Jeffries

Mrs M C Jenner

Joan

Barbara M Johnson

Harry & Judith Johnson

J A Johnson

R & K Jones

Shirley Jones

G R Jorden

Nicola Joule

Ruth, Bob, Laura & Rachel
   Jowett

Richard and Babeth Joy

Thomas Joy

David Judson

Mary Judson

Agnes Kane

Mrs L J Kaskiewicz

Tim Kay

John S Kaye

Shirley Kaye

Valerie Kaye

Jean & Richard Keighley

K J Keighley

Dr S W Ketteridge

H Kettlewell

In memory of Jack & Grace
   Kilburn

E B King

Ian King

Maureen King

D J Kirk
H M Kirk
Robert Kirk
Rev P Kirkham
B & J Kitching
Barbara Klempka
Mr John P Knight
J S Knight
Mrs Linda Knock

C P Lamb
Dr Glenn Lambert
Chris Lancaster
Renee Lapworth
Mr Howard Lawrence
Jacky Lawson
Donald Leach
J Leeming
John Lees
Patricia Anne Leggott
Geoff & Joyce Lester
Peter J Leveridge
A G & C A Liddle
M Lister
Miss M Lister
Gordon Littlewood
Baroness Lockwood
Mr C A Lodge
Mrs Marjorie Lomas
G A Longbottom
J Keith Lorrimer
Roy Lougheed
Sheila Loughlin
Liz Lowe
Philip Lowery
Anne & Chris Loy
Richard Lumley
Hilda Lunn
Mrs Pat Lupton
Mrs E M Lusby
Lyth

Mrs F M Machin
James K Machin
Mr Ritchie Macpherson
Peter Magoolagan
Janet Mallinson
Maureen & Dave Malyon
James G Marchbank
Denis Marsden
Carole J Marshall
Mrs Ena Marshall
Mrs Margaret Marson
Sheena Marx
Mary
David Mason

H T Mathew
G M Mattock
John Maud
Philip Maud
Jean - Jacques Mauvais
Anne McCarthy
Mr C McGarity
John A McLeod
J McPoskitt
Kevin K Melady
Stephen Mercer
Graham Metcalf
J B Metcalf
Everald Mary Metcalfe
Mrs P C Metcalfe
Paul Metcalfe
Mr P H Meyrick
Mollie Micklethwaite
P Middlebrook
Paul Milling
Derek Mills
D M Mills
P L Milner
David Mitchell
Douglas Mitchell
Moira Mitchell
Mr T S Mitchell
D R Moad
R Moffatt
Dorothy Moor
Liz Moore
John Moore
Ronnie Moore (U.S.A)
Katherine Moran
Theadore Moran
Dr A G Morgan
Maureen Morgan
Judith M Morris
Mr A J Morton
John Mounsey
A Muckalt
Raymond Mudd
Rosalind Muir
David Murray
Ruth Myers

Beryl E Naylor
John H W Neave
Doreen Needham (23.07.04)
F W Newlove
Terry Newsome
John Newton
Martha Newton
Peter Nicholas
C Nichols
George and Carol Nicholson

Ian Nicholson
Arthur Noble
Mr B P Nock
David Ian North
P W Nutt

Jeremy Oates
Isobel M O`Beirne
Nicholas C O`Flanagan
David I Oliver
Gary Oliver
Patricia Oliver
J Barry Osborne
Bob & Marie Oxtoby

Miss D Page
Susan Paish
Des Palmer
Jean Parker
Nevil H Parkinson
Vera Parkinson
Gladys Parr
V J Parsons
Joyce Patterson
Peter Pawley
Mrs N M Peach
Catherine M Peacock
Lin & Stan Pears (Newbold-Verdon)
John Pearson
Lesley Pearson
Simon Pearson
Evelyn Peel
Mollie Penny
R W Perkin
Josie Perryman
I Petch
Derek Phillips
Jeffrey Pickering
Donald Pimp of Harrogate - born there 1930
Steven J Plante
Susan M Platt
Ted Platt
Rita Pollard
Stephen Pope (Threshfield)
Leah Popkins - Wetherby
Ian Powell
D J Prescott
Mr John Prescott
A R Prestwich
Val Price
The Pritchard Family
Mr & Mrs Procter-Oswaldtwistle
Alex Proctor
Mrs D M Proctor

S J Purchon

C E Radcliffe
Stuart Raggett
John Rawlings
Patricia Rawson
Margaret V Rayner
Allan Read
Sheila M Read
R E Redman
Mary Redshaw
Brian & Lal Reed
David Morgan Rees
Mrs V Reeves
M Relton
Mrs A I Gwendolen Renton
M Revely
Kate Rhodes
Ronald Richards
R A Richford
Janet Ridgway
Audrey Riley
A Riley-Smith
Miss J Riley
Colin Roberts
Elisabeth Roberts
Mrs B Robinson
Edward Robinson
J Robinson
Miss J M Robinson
V S Robinson
John Robson
Maureen Rodgers
Mrs M Rodley
Mary Ronson
Jonathan Ropner
Richard Ross
Gordon Rowling
Jean Rushton

Eddie Sadler
Ken Sagar
Mr C J Sanderson
Philip Sanderson
S Sanderson
Hugh Sands
Derek W Sawyer
David J Sayer
Peter M Sayer
Michael J Scholey
Mr & Mrs K E Scott
P H E Scott
Gladys Scrimshaw
K & J Scruton
Evan Jack Seaman
Mrs B Sellers

Joan Sephton
R H Sharpe
Harry Shaw
Roger & Susan Shaw
Mike Shelton
F H Shepherd
Hannah Shimwell
Monica Simmons
Denis Simpson
E Charles Simpson
Marie Simpson
Norman Simpson
M G Slater
John Smailes
A J Smallwood
Brenda Smith
Mr C P Smith
Derek & Stella Smith
Harold Brook Smith
Jean M Smith
Dr Martyn Smith
Mary C Smith
R A Smith
S R Smith
Tony Smith
Viv Smith
William Smith
William J T Smith
N Spencer
The Stables
P H Stainthorpe
Gordon & Margaret Stanley
Winston Statham
S Stead
Mr A J Steele
A H Stocks
Pam Stott
P J S Stott
M Strachan
David A Strover
Evelyn Stubbs
John H Sture
Mrs S M Styles

Sue
Theo Sumners
Roy Sunderland
P D Sutcliffe
Jean and Roger Sykes
A J Sutcliffe
Jean H Swift

Tadcaster Grammar School
Peter Tait
P M Talbot
Alan Taylor
Clara Taylor
Clifford Taylor
M Taylor
Richard Tesseyman
Mr & Mrs K Thackray
Gillian R Thatcher
Eileen Thompson
Emma Thompson
Mrs Phyllis Thompson
Tessa Thorne
Noreen Thorp
Rev Kenneth Tibbetts
Simon Tidswell
Karen Tiller
James & Shirley Timiney
G Tinkler
Michael & Barbara Tobin
Alan Tooby
Leslie Tooby
George Tookey
Harold Toothill
W D Tovey
Jan & Norman Towler
Simon Townson
N Tristram
Miss Marion Troughton
R & M Trusler
N Tungate
David D Turner
Jonathan C D Turner
Paul J D Turner

N Tungate
R & M Trusler
R G Tyson

Philip Vaux
W J Veitch
Dr Donald Verity
W W Verity
Vivien

Dennis Waddle
David William Wade
Margaret Wadsley
David Edward Wadsworth
Mrs G R Wagstaff
Wakefield Girls` High School
Christine Walker
C J Walker
Jean Walker
Richard Walker
Gordon Walshaw
Anne Walton
Peter Walton
Ian Ward (Thorner)
W M Ward
Claire Warwick
Hazel Waters
Pat Waters
A S Watkinson
K Weatherall
B & J Weatherhead
Mr & Mrs P B Weatherhead
R & M Weatherhogg
C Webb
E & I Webster
Lodge Webster
Bob Weightman
Cherryl West
Mrs S Weymouth
S M Whincup
Jeanne White
Nick White
Janet Whitehead

Mrs J M Whitehead
Ian Whitelam
Mr Keith Whiteley
June Whitton
Mrs K Wilcox
Eric Wild
Mr & Mrs J Wiley
D A Wilkie (M.B.E)
S Wilkinson
Mrs Tracey Wilkinson
Joan M Williams
Barrie Williamson
Mrs G Willmott
Mervyn Wilmington
H Wilson
J Wilson
Mr K A Wilson
Lindsay Wilson
Sheila Wilson
Robert Wiltshire
A & I Windle
John R Winter
C Wood
Christopher John Wood
David Ronald Wood
Philip Wood
Roger Graham Wood
Ronald and Moira Wood
Andrew Woodall
In memory of G F &
   A Woodhead
M Woods
Gloria Worboys
Norman and Joyce
   Wordsworth
Vera & John Worledge
Mr & Mrs T G Wray
Michael J Wright
Robert & Wanda Wright

M G Yeadon
Mr & Mrs R W Young
M W I Yule